AN UNFORGETTABLE SALUTE

SKIRMISHES, BATTLEFIELDS, AND MAKING PEACE WITH MY FATHER

COL. JOHN R. GOUIN

iUniverse, Inc.
New York   Bloomington

An Unforgettable Salute
Skirmishes, Battlefields, and Making Peace with My Father

iUniverse books may be ordered through booksellers or by contacting:

iUniverse
1663 Liberty Drive
Bloomington, IN 47403
www.iuniverse.com
1-800-Authors (1-800-288-4677)

Because of the dynamic nature of the Internet, any Web addresses or links contained in this book may have changed since publication and may no longer be valid. The views expressed in this work are solely those of the author and do not necessarily reflect the views of the publisher, and the publisher hereby disclaims any responsibility for them.

ISBN: 978-1-4502-3979-0 (sc)
ISBN: 978-1-4502-3980-6 (dj)
ISBN: 978-1-4502-3981-3 (ebook)

Library of Congress Control Number: 2010908936

Printed in the United States of America

iUniverse rev. date: 09/27/2010

This book is based on the true-life exploits of Col John R. Gouin. The names of certain characters have been changed in order to protect their privacy.

This book is dedicated to my mother, Theresa F. Gouin, who unconditionally loved and tolerated my father. She is to be admired for her perseverance, love, and no-quit attitude. She truly stood by her husband for fifty-seven years, for better or worse.

It is through her courage and inspiration that I have been able to put forth the words and thoughts in this book to help me and others understand that there is no greater bond than family, despite the hardships. It is a true bond of the heart, regardless of flesh or blood, that allows us to endure as family through the most difficult and painful circumstances.

She truly has proven to me that the words "I quit!" are not in her vocabulary, and her attitude encouraged me to follow her example.

There are many rivers that we cross in our lifetime, but unfortunately, some of those rivers just don't have bridges.

~ **J. R. Gouin**

Contents

Acknowledgments

I thank God for providing me with courage and inspiration in paving the pathway to completing this book. Writing *An Unforgettable Salute* was extremely painful at times and helped me heal the deep-seated wounds that I have carried for many years. I hope this book may shine some light on those who suffer with living conditions far worse than what I experienced. I wanted to bring even a small amount of comfort and guidance to help the abused understand that they are not alone. I thank him every day that I have a wonderful, supportive family that has stood by me during the worst of times. God has given me the ability to love with all my heart and to look past worldly possessions as a measure of love.

I would like to acknowledge my sister, Carol A. Murphy, for providing me with her recollections of our childhood and the courage to describe the last few moments she experienced with our dad as he passed.

I would like to thank the U.S. Army and Special Forces for allowing me the opportunity to believe in myself and develop vision and confidence. The army instilled in me the guidance and discipline needed to accomplish any task, no matter how physically demanding or mentally challenging.

Special Thanks

To Rusty Fisher for his assistance in writing this book.
To Margie Dane for her assistance in writing this book.

Introduction

For as long as I can remember, I've always dreamed of writing a book filled with emotion and overflowing with passion. I wanted to write about something that would cause a change for the better in someone's life, especially my own. Even if just one person were positively affected by reading what I wrote, I would consider myself an accomplished writer who made a difference.

A burning desire to write about something with substance sparked my desire to warm the heart and soul of my readers. I was determined to make them feel they were right there beside me, experiencing every powerful detail I encountered.

Finding the perfect topic to write about was the most difficult aspect of starting the book. I wanted to write about something positive, but to write about what we, as a family, swept under the carpet was unimaginable. Some of my best friends and relatives were clueless about what happened in our home on Friday and Saturday nights.

We made our best effort to hide our problem, but I am sure some of our neighbors heard the screaming, the cries, and the breaking glass on weekends. Maybe some of the neighbors knew what was going on in the Gouin household; then again, maybe they did not. In any event, what happened then is in the past and is now part of this book.

Since we grew up on the receiving end of abusive behavior, we assumed it was a normal occurrence in every family; maybe they never talked about it either. As a child, I had difficulty understanding the idea that we were abused or even poor. All I knew was that violence could break out at any moment in our home and that I needed to tread softly.

During our early years, we never discussed the problem openly as a family. We simply coped and adjusted to the fearful lifestyle as best we could. Only later, when we became adults, did we revisit the matter. Even without the presence of my father, the apprehension lingered. He had permanently instilled fear into us all, which churned like sour milk in the pits of our stomachs. When Dad walked into the apartment and slammed the door behind him, it was his signal for us to cringe in fear.

I often questioned my reasons for writing this book and the possible repercussions that could come from exposing the truth. I wrote this book with the intention of cleansing, healing, and purging my soul of the past; I did not mean to air our dirty laundry or provide fuel for hometown gossip. Despite what is written in this book, I have no purposeful intention to degrade or embarrass my father's memory, my mother, or my siblings. What is recounted here occurred in my life and comes from the darkest corner of my memory and the deepest part of my heart. It has been extremely difficult at times to put my thoughts on paper and relive many of the things that happened to my family and me.

Writing this book has helped me take a second look and identify my real self, my strengths and weaknesses. After stepping back and looking at it from a reader's perspective, I was surprised to see that my character developed thanks to my mother's inspiration and my dad's behavior. Who I am was ultimately shaped by my dad, my mother, my family, and my environment. The sequence of events that unfolded in my life played an important role in my success, and I am extremely thankful that life turned out for the best for all of us. I can speculate on what could have or should have happened in our family, but I will leave that to our creator.

A psychiatrist might think about this differently, describing what happened in medical terms and jargon, but what difference does it make? I am sure many people will question some of my comments, my perspective, or even my motive in writing this book, but that is okay. I accept and welcome these opinions. I donned a military uniform for over thirty-three years to defend our right to say what we please.

I believe that success is measured by a positive end state, reached by accomplishing a task or achieving a goal. It may have been a rocky road, but

I think my mother and siblings would agree that the result has been favorable for all of us. As you read this book, please understand that nobody is perfect; sometimes the road to hell is paved with good intentions.

Despite my dad's shortcomings, I think he always had good intentions for his family, but I will not excuse his behavior. He obviously had serious anger management issues that surfaced when he consumed alcohol, fueling the fire for his uncontrollable fits of rage.

I know the difference between abuse and negative reinforcement. I contend that there is nothing wrong with an occasional old-fashioned spanking, either publicly or privately. Punching, beating, and doing far worse to a child are clearly unacceptable. However, how many of us are witnesses to our own abuse and never raise a word until it is too late? It makes you stop and think.

We are not the only family that has ever been abused, nor will ours be the last. Countless families receive or have received unimaginable abuse far worse than mine. It may be easy for me to say, but they need to seek professional help before it is too late. The abuse we endured could have been far worse under the circumstances; we were simply fortunate by the grace of God.

Many readers may raise the question, "Why is he discussing his family's dirty laundry now, after all these years?" I was compelled to tell a story about the love/hate relationship between my abusive, alcoholic father and me; I wanted to explore how it shaped my personality and how I wondered what could have been with the alcohol removed from the equation. There are numerous stories to be told regarding parental alcohol abuse, but many of the abused prefer to leave their stories buried and forgotten.

As simple as it may sound, at the time we didn't let anyone know what was happening behind closed doors. Loyalty in our family was a sacred bond that was never broken despite the ugliness that occurred in our household. Maybe we didn't know how to escape the misery or feared my dad's reprisals. There are thousands of families asking themselves the same question. Sometimes they act too late, and the consequences are tragic and often fatal.

Many families like mine keep their daily abuse quiet. I hope this book will draw some attention to the silent side of abuse and help other families seek the support that can make a difference in their lives.

Regardless of why the abuse occurs, whether it is alcohol, drugs, financial stress, or lack of anger control, help is available. During the sixties, there were minimal resources. It is highly likely that we never knew where to seek help. Then again, maybe we were simply too afraid to speak up.

Therefore, as you read this book, do not look at my father as an evil or cruel man but rather as a confused man with good intentions who was blinded by his explosive temperament and addiction to alcohol.

Chapter 1: *Backwash*
(Iraq, September 2005)

This is a pain I mostly hide, but ties of blood, or seed endure, and even now I feel inside the hunger for his outstretched hand, a man's embrace to take me in, the need for just a word of praise.

~ Jimmy Carter

Strapped into the backseat of a Blackhawk helicopter, I could feel the arid heat from the backwash of the rotor blades blasting across my sweaty face. The temperature on any given day could run as high as 125 degrees; there was no escaping the heat. I felt like I was sitting under an enormous hair dryer, despite the fact that I was drenched in sweat from head to toe.

My body armor, which weighed nearly forty-five pounds, along with a Kevlar helmet, a CamelBak canteen, a basic load of ammunition, and assorted survival gear, intensified the heat. This was the military equivalent of wrapping a potato in tin foil and baking it. My eyes were already dry and itchy from the desert heat. The blast of wind from the rotor blades stirred the fine, powdery particles of sand into the helicopter, making my eyes even more red, raw, and irritated. My lips were cracking and my mouth was parched, but the thought of drinking water out of my CamelBak canteen, water that would be roughly the same temperature as the desert, barely crossed my mind. I had no appetite for hot water soup that day.

With a loaded weight of approximately twenty-two thousand pounds, the Blackhawk was surprisingly agile, flying at speeds of approximately 125 knots or 140 miles per hour. Its crew of four and one passenger kept constant vigil for enemy activity as they flew fifty to one hundred feet over the eternally shifting sea of sand below. The first time I saw one of these magnificent flying creatures, I was in awe. I stared at it like a high school kid checking out the latest Corvette. Yet the first thought that came to my mind was that the name of this awesome machine didn't quite match the sleek, powerful outer shell of this amazing creation.

The reference to the predator hawk was obvious, but a Blackhawk in flight brings to life more than nature. Rotors at the ready; the nonreflective, flat black skin, scaly and tough; a shape as sleek and aerodynamic as a heat-seeking Sidewinder missile—it looked more like an insect than a bird. It resembles nothing more than a well-groomed metal wasp. Watching one tragically downed in combat is to witness man's insignificance in the grand scheme of things; another insect squashed on history's windshield. Watching several in flight is to see the awesome wonder of man's modern marvel of a swarm in action.

There I was, inside that swarm, hitching a ride from one of those well-groomed metal wasps, feeling completely anonymous, inexplicably numb, and extremely vulnerable. At fifty-one years old, I didn't feel fully prepared to go to war, even though I had over twenty-eight years of military training, ranging from Special Forces Sniper School to the parachute training school at Fort Benning, Georgia. My infantry training as a private helped me understand the foundation of the entire military, including the mechanics of the foot soldier. No matter what kind of support he or she gets, eventually a private will have to kick in a door, walk out on point in a patrol, and secure the ground he or she just took from the bad guys.

Sometimes my sense of humor and easygoing personality suggested that I was a pushover; but when I said something, I said what I meant, and I stood by what I said. My previous military and civilian medical background made me a perfect asset for a new assignment with the 228th Combat Support Hospital and its home station in San Antonio, Texas. Now I was accompanying them on their deployment to Iraq.

The constant daily threat of surface-to-air missiles and small-arms fire kept me on my guard, wondering if my end would come from a shoulder-fired, rocket-propelled grenade, better known as an RPG.

Despite the fiery images constantly played on TV for the anxious crowd back home, I found that the fighter pilot ratio of "99 percent boredom, 1 percent sheer terror" was true for the modern soldier as well. At this point, I wasn't sure which was worse.

Like most soldiers, during the boring times, I looked out over the barren Iraqi desert and reminisced about my family, my job as a respected podiatric surgeon, and the very comfortable civilian lifestyle I'd left back home. Some parts of my life had already started to disappear by now: the office pallor, the early signs of the middle-age spread, the mornings free of aches and pains. But other parts were still very real to me.

Like a phantom limb, I couldn't shake the expectation that each morning I'd rise to find myself at home, safe in my large California-style bed. In my memory, awakening to a blaring Bose stereo alarm clock was no longer an annoyance—not when compared to the sound of the morning Muslim call to prayer. I missed having my beautiful wife, Leslie, near me as I brushed the sleep from my eyes; I missed a good morning lick in the face from our twelve-pound cockapoo, Gus. It always took me a few moments to readjust to the nomadic, desert lifestyle I'd slowly grown accustomed to, a lifestyle that included the endless threat of unexpected violence from improvised explosive devices (IEDs) and mortar and rocket attacks. True relaxation was impossible, and REM sleep was a thing of the past.

Even though I'd adjusted, I couldn't forget about my life back home—a life most people could only dream about. I lived in a two-story Mediterranean-style home with beige stucco, a dark red tiled roof, and a gorgeous view of the Gulf of Mexico. When I closed my eyes, I envisioned the cool, fresh water of our blue lagoon pool cascading from the rock waterfall. The lush, tropical backyard laced with palm trees, hibiscus, and bougainvillea plants was my refuge, my paradise, my home—and now over a half a world away. I had volunteered for Operation Iraqi Freedom and, on Christmas Day 2004, left behind a wonderful family, a beautiful home, and a lucrative medical practice. As the rest of the world opened presents and spent the day complaining about relatives while surrounded by the aroma of baking turkey and pies, I was embarking on the first leg of a journey that would lead me to ground zero of the fight against terrorism.

The most peculiar aspect about that Christmas was that it snowed on Christmas Eve and continued through the early morning. Rising from my warm, comfortable bed, I was surprised to see a winter wonderland in the backyard. A blanket of snow several inches deep is not so peculiar if you live in one of the northern states; but it had been nearly one hundred years since the city of Corpus Christi had had that much snow. Was this rare, cold, shimmering covering of snow a teasing reminder of the grizzly heat I was about to endure for the next year?

I repeatedly asked myself why a fifty-one-year-old man would volunteer to go to a combat zone, leaving behind everything he had struggled to achieve. I had come such a long way since my family's days of poverty, when we lived in a housing project. I no longer needed to put cardboard in my worn-out shoes. Why would I leave my gorgeous wife, who promised to patiently wait for me in our beautiful home on North Padre Island, Texas? Why would I leave a successful medical practice and risk my life to come to a place like *this*? Why would I trade in civilian luxury for military issue? Why would I trade an office full of loyal patients and staff to suit up and ship out? Perhaps most puzzling of all, why would I trade personal security and safety for violence and mayhem?

There was more to my sense of obligation and service to my country than the obvious. I accepted the fact that there were thousands of soldiers, civilians, and families who had already made the ultimate sacrifice; my service would be only a small contribution. I would be making an insignificant personal sacrifice, especially compared to those who had served before me and to those who were about to do the same.

I may have been groomed for this mission since childhood. It is said that the ghosts of our past haunt us until our days on this planet are done. These spirits are constantly nipping at our heels and looming in the shadows, ever present, no matter what our triumphs or failures may be. Had my past finally caught up with me? Had my own personal demons followed me to the desert? Had they, perhaps, sent me there in the first place?

I became lost in thought, hypnotized by the sound of the helicopter blades. I was no longer conscious of my surroundings, which was dangerous in a combat zone. The constant hum of the engine slowly faded, and I began to drift back to my childhood, those long-lost but not forgotten days of violence, poverty, fear, and devotion. As I left one world, a vivid, frightful picture of a previous world gradually emerged. I began to think about my father …

Chapter 2: *Saturday Night Fights*

I am absolutely sure that a lot of Daddy anger has more to do with unrealized dreams than with messy rooms. Trust me. You're not really angry at your kids. You're angry at somebody else, somebody who is a far less distinguished person than he dreamed of being.

~ **Hugh O'Neill**

My childhood world could not have been any further removed from Iraq than if it had been written in the pages of a classic novel. I began to relive the story of my past as it unfolded in my mind and overpowered my hot, sweaty, sandy reality. What slowly emerged was a scene as all-American as watching the Red Sox play at Fenway Park on a bright summer afternoon; or biting into a piece of homemade apple pie with vanilla ice cream melting and dripping over the sides; or smelling popcorn and cotton candy at a Fourth of July parade while standing on the curb in a small New England town, waving an American flag. It all seems so picture-perfect—or so you'd think.

It was autumn 1965, a typical fall evening in New England, the kind perfectly captured by a Norman Rockwell painting. The air was brisk, and the colorful dry leaves rustled in a cool evening breeze as the sun began to set. The harvest moon reared its bright orange head with its mysterious Mona Lisa smile.

A small, historical industrial city in northern Rhode Island, consisting mostly of French Canadian immigrants, was the center of my childhood and young adulthood. My parents were lifelong inhabitants of Woonsocket and rarely ventured out from their comfort zone and meager income. Although my parents spoke fluent French, my dad refused to allow his children speak it because of the stigma associated with being a "Canuck." Despite his French Canadian background, he felt there was a negative association with migrant workers and speaking French.

These migrant workers were mostly employed in the once-bustling textile industry that had flourished at the turn of the century. They continued to work at the factories until the early seventies. Now, the mostly vacant red-brick textile plants had broken, boarded-up windows; they would soon be renovated into affordable elderly residences and condominiums.

The remnants of the cobblestone streets were dotted with beautiful maple, elm, and oak trees. The steel rails from the trolley cars tracks were barely visible, buried under many layers of asphalt-laden black top. The weathered gas lamps and hitching posts on the once-bustling Main Street were long gone and almost forgotten. Finding anything like that today is rare, except in preserved historic towns like Newport, Rhode Island, or Fredericksburg, Texas.

I meandered past the apartment houses and brightly colored trees that lined our street, inching my way to the large, dingy yellow, rundown tenement building we called home. My mouth watered as I inhaled the aromas of ethnic foods wafting from the homes and apartments. The smell of fried chicken, home-baked bread, peppers, onions, and sautéed garlic and sausage aroused my voracious appetite, as it would with any athletic twelve-year-old boy.

There were five other families living in the three-story wooden building, which was typical for low-income families living in this neighborhood. It was built in the early 1920s to accommodate the massive influx of migrant workers into the city. The building consisted of two columns of three single-family apartment homes stacked on top of each other. The dilapidated building was in poor condition, but its collapsing front porches and peeling exterior paint made the rent very affordable. There were no other reasonably priced options for a family of five in the area. Despite the conditions, it was better than living back in the housing project.

Inside the apartment, there was only one very small bathroom with a claw-foot tub and a handheld shower. In a family of five, there were many arguments over the use of this essential room.

An old chrome dinette set, with scratches on the imitation blue marble-top table, filled the kitchen. On the seat cushions were curled edges of tape that restrained the cotton lining protruding through the plastic covering. The set, stylish in the sixties, had seen better days, but it served its purpose. The dining table is usually a gathering place for families, where they break bread and share their stories about the day. In our home, however, at any moment it could become a place of intense fear and anxiety for the inattentive or foolishly brave.

Dad had his own place at the table. The entire family understood that Dad was the only person allowed to occupy the special place of regality. He was the breadwinner, the head of the household, but we all knew that my mother kept the family together. He laid down the law, and daring to defy that law resulted in a guaranteed slap to the back of the head. It was an expected consequence of committing such a heinous violation.

Dad strategically positioned himself closest to the stove so he had easy access to the food when my mother was not available to get up and cater to his needs. More importantly, Dad had a very low tolerance for cold. Sitting close to the source of heat during the colder months gave him the warmth he desperately desired.

The closet-sized pantry at the side of the kitchen offered limited work and storage space. Mom did the best she could with the ragged wooden storage cabinets and the four-foot-long linoleum countertop. This narrow room forced Mom to optimize every inch of workspace.

There were only two sources of heat in the apartment. The main source was the bulky black-and-white cast iron Kalamazoo gas stove, which had a heater attached. The other was a small gas space heater in the living room. The absence of central heat made the New England winters miserably cold. I would stand by the side of the stove, warm my backside, and then quickly run into bed. Having a warmed butt and extra blankets made the night tolerable, but getting out of bed in the morning was unbearable.

We always looked forward to the short, pleasant summers and the moderately cooler autumns. The apartment lacked air-conditioning and ceiling fans, but one or two oscillating tabletop fans made hot humid weather more acceptable.

As a child, I hardly knew that I was living in a low-income family. What we had was all we ever knew. Life seemed normal to me, despite what went on behind our closed doors, and even that sometimes seemed normal. Nevertheless, the living conditions were far better than at the last apartment we lived in, at the nearby housing project. There were no foul odors of cat urine reeking from the crawl space. There were no hookers with their revolving door of visitors. There were no screams for help or bloody beatings going on in the adjacent apartments. However, those screams and beatings were now beginning to happen in the new place we called home.

The walk home might have seemed like a gauntlet for some kids, but for the neighborhood kids, who didn't know the difference, it was normal. However, going home was much different for my siblings, my mom, and me. In a ritual of fear and apprehension, I would stop at the bottom of the apartment stairs, glare up at the door, and wonder what was lurking inside for the evening. What was in store for me just beyond those creaky old wooden doors? I would take a deep breath. The hair on the back of my neck would stand up, and my heart rate would accelerate. I would drag myself up that single flight of stairs, step by step, for what seemed to be an eternity.

Football practice had just finished on that Friday evening, and, like most boys in the neighborhood, I delayed going home. Hanging out on the park wall and gazing at the cool evening sky allowed me an opportunity to escape for a little while from the fear of reality.

I had a vague idea that one day I would wear an NFL jersey. I visualized charging onto the field of one of America's most famous stadiums, such as Lambeau Field in Green Bay, Wisconsin, or Soldier Field in Chicago, Illinois, amidst thousands of cheering fans. It didn't matter what jersey or what team; I just needed to be an NFL player. From a very early age, I was determined to wear a professional jersey. I was willing to make all the necessary sacrifices, endure the hard work ahead, and reach my goal.

I wanted to play preteen football between the ages of ten and twelve. I played extremely well at age ten, but there was a problem: I was simply too big and exceeded the height and weight requirements for my age group. After playing that one year, I sat out the next two years because of my size. Had I just faced my first disappointment in an early football career, or was it simply a blessing, allowing me to gain strength, speed, and maturity in order to play in the next-higher league?

My dad persuaded me to try out for Junior League Football, the next level up from preteen. It was at his intimidating request that I walked to the local park on a bright fall morning and signed up for tryouts. I was much bigger than most kids my age, naturally strong and very agile; but, because of my size, the coaches channeled me into playing the offensive line. I was to become a blocker, the unsung hero of football. I had no problem making a team, and I soon learned that I enjoyed participating in the hard-hitting contact sport.

Dad was quite familiar with football, especially in the day when the players did not have facemasks on their helmets. He had firsthand experience with the sport, which involved a life-changing event and a great disappointment in his life. He'd dreamed that he himself would one day make it to the pros. However, those hopes were shattered one cold, wet Saturday morning during a local semipro football game in front of hundreds of fans.

As a teenager, Dad played semipro football for a popular local team called the Red Raiders. When he was nineteen, the scouts already considered him an NFL prospect. He had all the necessary physical attributes for professional football, but he was lacking one major ingredient: experience. He knew he needed to gain this essential piece to play in the pros, and that piece was the Red Raiders. He practiced hard in the evenings and worked out long hours while still working in the daytime at a local factory making rubber boats for the military.

He met and married my mother, Theresa, who was twenty-two. Within a few short months she was expecting their first child, Michael. Dad was able to provide a comfortable lifestyle for his new family; they lived in a quiet neighborhood duplex apartment down the street from my mother's family. Everything seemed to be going according to their ideal plan: job, family, children on the way, and the potential for greater football success with the NFL.

Then the unthinkable happened, the nightmare of every athlete. That day, the distinctively loud crack of what sounded like a limb snapping off a tree echoed across the football field. My father's football career was instantly over. His right leg was severely broken in several places, crippling his chances of playing in the NFL. His leg was shattered, along with his dreams and the affluent lifestyle that could have followed for him and his family. From that day, they began to lead the impoverished life they'd have for many years to come.

He was no longer able to play football or even capable of bringing home any form of a decent paycheck. Having a pregnant wife who was unable to work didn't help matters. He and his family were now in serious financial trouble, and the elevated stress levels were about to lead them into a world they had never dreamed of. They were forced to use all their savings on the surgeries Dad needed, even though that money had been earmarked for a future home. The doctors' visits and rehabilitation of his fractured leg quickly depleted their cash reserves. Meanwhile, their first child was about to be born. There were no Social Security benefits, worker's compensation, food stamps, or any other kind of federal assistance available to them other than affordable low-income housing. Jack and Theresa's once-promising outlook for their life had vanished. It was gone, all gone. They had no choice but to move to a housing project dedicated to low-income families and stand in line for powdered milk, eggs, cheese, and lard, a chore that would become a weekly norm for them.

When I learned about my dad's mishap many years later, my compassion inspired me to make my father's dream come true, with his assistance. Whatever it took to make him proud and happy was my ultimate end-state. However, there was a darker side within the Gouin household, a side we kept hidden within the family for many years.

I was a normal twelve-year-old American boy with big hopes and dreams. One day I would make it to the NFL, taking our family out of that old apartment and low-income neighborhood. I'd take them away from the loud, clattering noises of the factory and the foul smell of carbon and sulfur from the steel foundry across the street. Like most adolescent boys, I was straddling the worlds of boyhood and adulthood, on my way to becoming a man who wanted a better quality of life for my family and myself.

Our surroundings were as dismal as the crisp fall New England afternoon was vibrant. Shimmering leaves of ginger, auburn, and gold dangled and eventually floated to the ground from the bare trees that lined the neighborhood streets. What seemed so peaceful outside stood in sharp contrast to what was happening within the depressing walls of our family's latest address.

Fatigued from attending school, practicing in the evening, and dreading the night, I wearily climbed the stairs to our rundown apartment. We had lived there only a year or two, having moved away from the row house in the low-income, government-subsidized housing project. Living there gave you an education that Yale, Harvard, or Brown could never offer. I learned fast and hard, earning an unrecognized degree in street smarts. I had to be tough, strong, and smart, or I paid a price, especially when I walked to school through the local public park. There was no way around it. I had to know how to defend myself, or at least know how to fake it. Otherwise, I could lose my jacket, what little lunch money I carried, or even my shoes, if they didn't have holes in them.

My shoes were usually not new, and I didn't need to worry about the neighborhood bully wanting to steal them. Coming home and explaining to Dad how I lost my shoes was inviting brutal consequences. He grew angry not so much at my coming home without them but at the fact that I'd allowed someone else to take them. Moving out of the projects gave me a false sense of confidence that we were moving up on the social scale.

When the soles of my shoes wore out, I knew it wasn't time to ask for a new pair. It was time to be humble and creative. I would look for an apartment that was under renovation and rummage through the trash barrels. Once I found a sturdy piece of linoleum, I trimmed it into the shape of my shoes. I applied a little glue and slipped the new "sole" inside to make my shoes last a little longer. But it wasn't the shoes I was worried about that night. It was going home.

As darkness filled the sky, I climbed the stairs and approached the back porch cautiously. I carefully peered through the kitchen window, studying an all-too-familiar scene: my mother standing in the kitchen preparing dinner. She was the perfect neighbor who everyone wanted next door.

She often assisted the little old woman who lived alone in the adjacent apartment with her laundry. She would watch the neighbors' kids for a while and pick things up at the grocery store for anyone who couldn't get out of the house. My mother was the kind of person who would do just about anything for anyone. She always took the time to listen to what people had to say. Her pleasant demeanor attracted people to her, and they enjoyed being around her. She was a beautiful woman with well-defined Italian features, dark hair, an olive complexion, and beautiful brown eyes. She had a gentle touch and a soothing voice around her children. She displayed patience with her husband's behavior, especially when he came home late from a night on the town. She was always prepared to make him a meal, regardless of the time. Mom unconditionally loved her children, as most mothers would, and I sometimes looked at her with an inquisitive smile, wondering if she was a saint.

Though she walked three miles to work every day, she never complained about the distance or the weather. A stop in the small Catholic church to pray was part of her daily routine. My mother never told me why she made her daily pilgrimages, but I knew it was to pray for something better, maybe a better way of life.

Entering through the back door and tossing my shoulder pads on the kitchen floor, I asked, "What's for dinner, Mom?"

She replied, "Your favorite: hot dog soup! How was practice?"

"Good. You know, Mom, I'm trying really hard so one day I can make it to the pros. I want to buy us a beautiful home!"

"Well," she said, her face showing a weary hint of gratitude combined with her desire to teach her son a lesson, "I appreciate that, but you need to do well in school first! You can't get to the pros without going to college, and how do you get to college? Don't make the same mistake I did."

In her eyes was a mixture of happiness and despair, which confused me; yet somehow I knew exactly what she was thinking. Mom dropped out of school in eleventh grade to get a job. Of course, in the early 1940s, during World War II, saving some money at seventeen was a good choice for a girl and quite common at the time. The women's liberation movement was still in its infancy, and even if it had been all the rage, her circumstances would have kept her out of the loop. Nevertheless, she dropped out of high school, even though she'd already been selected for a full scholarship at a local school of design.

Several years later, I found out the truth: my mother had been forbidden by her father to take the scholarship. Her place was in the home, as was preordained by her "old school" Sicilian father, Giuseppe. He left Sicily as a seventeen-year-old and never looked back; he was a firm believer that a woman was meant to be the backbone of the household, the matriarch around whom all family life flourished.

My mother's life choices were already made by her heavily accented Sicilian father; her destiny was preshaped and her life preplanned. She was an intelligent woman despite her level of education. Committed to family and her marriage vows, she was destined to a life of contrast: happiness with her children and misery with the man she loved.

"I know, I know," I finally said, not wanting to cause her any more grief.

Our conversation ended abruptly when the front door slammed loudly shut. We were startled, immediately turning our heads and looking at each other. It was a distinctive sound that we'd heard, and feared, many times before, usually on Saturday nights but sometimes on Friday nights. Exchanging looks of surprise and apprehension, we anticipated the worst but were nonetheless hopeful that the evening would be kind to us.

In retrospect, I don't know why the two of us were so hopeful about having a pleasant family night, something we hadn't had in a while. The odds were far from being in our favor, and many previous weekends had set the precedent by now. Nevertheless, both Mom and I were hopeful dreamers and not gamblers, especially on the weekends.

What did odds mean to a pair like us?

As Dad walked through the door, I quickly glanced into his eyes and knew right away the kind of evening that was in store for me and my mother. His eyes were red and glassy, and he looked like a different man than the one who'd left for work that morning. The familiar smell of alcohol and smoke on his clothes was a dead giveaway that we should expect trouble.

Worse than the tell-tale glassy eyes or the smell of beer and cigarettes that wafted off my Dad as he bounced off the walls and pounded into the front room was the absolute silence that greeted his entry. There were no good-natured hellos or even a desultory "I'm home." It was as if a virus had slipped into the house, penetrating the laughter and conversation and bursting it like a pin pressed too closely against a balloon.

The stillness that accompanied Dad's homecoming was not that of a thoughtful philosopher; instead, it was the side effect of a man lost to his own anger. He was a victim of his own silent, stalking rage, and he hated the world for his misfortune. I often thought about what angered my father so intensely and wondered if it was his lost opportunity to make it in football. I would never really know.

If only his bark were worse than his bite! But Dad's body matched the violent nature of his discouraged, resentful, and frustrated mind. He was tall, slightly balding, and rugged, a physically powerful man with years of bottled-up rage inside him. His nickname was "Jack," after the famous boxer Jack Dempsey, because of his toughness, size, and ability to box well. He did his best to live up to his reputation, both on the street and within the confines of his home. Dad was undoubtedly the boss of the family, and there were no mistakes made about it: everyone in it knew it all too well.

Dad had grown up in a low-income neighborhood as well, and he'd never had any desire to move out. He quit school in eighth grade and went to work.

He had no confidence in himself and little ambition, motivation, or drive; maybe he'd never had anyone to mentor him or help him set lifelong goals and objectives. Whatever the reason, he was quite content with his job at the local hospital as an orderly, and he spent his free time officiating high school football and gambling at the local bars.

More than anything else that puzzled me about my Dad was his lack of ambition. On the other hand, my mother spent most of her evenings dreaming of a better way of life. My younger sister, Carol, understood early on that using her brain was the best way to improve her position in life. She was tall for her age and had long, beautiful, thick brown hair with shimmering auburn highlights, which dangled down to the base of her spine. Her pretty hazel eyes matched her mood or whatever she was wearing for the day. In a green shirt, she had green eyes; in a blue dress, she had blue eyes. Carol was quiet but extremely grateful that she was never the target of Dad's ferocious rage. Meanwhile, I began practicing day and night to achieve my goal of wearing that NFL jersey and obtaining the better life it implied. My drive, determination, and ambition were there, but fatherly guidance and mentorship were missing.

What possessed my father to be so content and complacent with what little we had? More accurately, what was missing? What did he not have or want? Did he just give up on life after his injury? Of course, contentment and happiness are two different things. While Dad did little to improve his station in life, he still lived his life as an unhappy man. He never seemed happy except when he spent his evenings at a local bar, making extra money by playing cards, or when he officiated football on weekends.

As he staggered over to the kitchen table and pulled out his chair, I lowered my head and sat perfectly still, trying to avoid eye contact. Hoping to head off the inevitable fireworks, I said in a low, fearful voice, "Hi, Dad."

The kitchen was morbidly quiet; you could hear, as the saying went, a pin drop. There was a moment of silence. It wasn't the moment of silence that kids are accustomed to adhering to before the start of a school day. It was more like a funereal silence, the dreadful hesitation that accompanies the dead. Dad's deep, commanding voice suddenly broke the silence, causing me to jump. In a loud voice he asked, "What's the matter with you, and why are you always moping?"

My intense fear prevented me from saying a single word; my hands trembled, and my heart raced. My body was a picture of the "fight or flight response" I'd learned about in school, and I immediately assumed a defensive posture. How could anyone possibly answer a question for which the questioner was the answer? Knowing there was no answer that would prevent a battle, I merely sat there, cowering, wishing, praying, and hoping for the moment to blow over. My moping was related to my fear of Dad's wrath, and he didn't care what anyone else in the family thought. I was caught between loving my father and fearing him when he had that look in his eye.

How could Dad possibly confuse cowering with moping? How could he be so blinded by his own hatred that he couldn't realize that his son was cowering and moping because of him?

Since we never knew what would set him off, we stuck to noncontroversial subjects in our conversations. I tried to make small talk about the news, grades (good, of course), and winning sports scores, or I praised Dad for his job. Everything else was off-limits, and avoiding other topics was the best way of avoiding a confrontation or a beating. We all knew better than to anger him for any reason, intentional or accidental.

When I didn't rise to take the bait, my father simply stared at me and said, "How was practice?"

Hoping to keep the domestic scene calm, I said in an excited yet apprehensive voice, "Good! I'm really trying hard. I want to be a good football player. I want to make it to the pros someday!"

Dad slowly lifted his head from his soup bowl, glared at me with his reddened eyes, and said suggestively, "You need to know about the football officials too!" Dad was a football official for high school and the local youth football league, working weekend games for an additional source of income. Dad usually spent any extra money he earned on beer and gambling at the local bar. Unfortunately, we never saw any of that money.

Dad's remark, which might have been considered simply an offhand comment at any other family's table, was a test in our house. It was an opportunity for the alpha male to prove his dominance in the family hierarchy. My mother and I could see and feel the tension elevate, and we knew we should expect an explosion of rage at any minute. This one was not going to be pretty. He gave me an angry look, like Jack Nicholson's evil glare in *The Shining*, and asked, "What's the difference between the referee and the umpire on the football field?"

My heart sank like a ton of bricks. I should have known this one, but I didn't. To this rookie football player, all the officials were referees dressed in black and white stripes. *They were just referees.* "I don't know, Dad," I finally replied in a low, quivering voice. Intimidating my father was not on my list of favorite things to do; but how could a twelve-year-old boy intimidate a grown man?

"What do you mean, you don't know?" Dad asked. His voice began to increase in intensity and ferociousness. He might have been a civilian, but he had a drill sergeant's voice. When he yelled, his voice reverberated through my body as though I were being strafed with gunfire or blasted by a grenade.

"I'm just being frank, Dad," I said with a shudder, my throat parched. I knew I'd made a devastating mistake. A young adolescent making that kind of comment was considered disrespectful, and I was about to receive another lesson about respect. I was also about to discover that corporal punishment in our home was meted out for minor offenses. Eventually, I'd learn to keep my mouth shut and speak only when spoken to—and that my ideas were unimportant. This key event would split me in two. I had little or no confidence in social interactions with other kids my age. On the other hand, I was completely confident on the football field, punishing other twelve-year-old kids mercilessly. I badly wanted what any kid wanted—to be able to talk to my father without being afraid that I'd offend him and have to suffer the consequences.

"Frank, my ass!" Dad shouted, the boom in his voice foreshadowing the violence that was about to flow from his huge fists. All hell was about to break out. Dad slowly pushed himself away from the table. He stood up and gave me a demonic look.

Slowly lifting my head from my soup bowl, I timidly looked into Dad's eyes and knew what to expect. My eyes immediately filled with tears, my heart rate increased, and my hands continued to tremble. I watched this immense wall of flesh and muscle reach for a pepper shaker—a ten-inch-tall, solid oak pepper shaker that had been last year's Christmas gift from a relative. I knew what to expect and did what any kid would have done.

I attempted to make a lifesaving break from the table, but there was no escaping the powerful grip of my father's massive hand when he grabbed my left arm. Struggling to resist the forthcoming onslaught was futile. I peered over my left shoulder and glimpsed the downward trajectory of the pepper shaker. I frantically tried to protect myself by putting my other arm behind the back of my head. I immediately felt and heard the crack of the pepper shaker over my back and shoulders. My dad was smart enough to know not to leave any facial bruises or marks that would taint his image at the local bar and around the neighborhood.

"Dad, stop! Please!" I begged and cried as I struggled to break free. The harder I tried to pull away, the harder I was beaten. My mother cried and pleaded with her husband to stop, but he turned and looked at her with his anger-glazed eyes and refocused his assault on her. He screamed at her and blamed her for their son's insolent behavior. He then delivered a flurry of blows to her arms and back as she unsuccessfully attempted to protect herself.

As Dad brutally attacked Mom, I seized the opportunity to recover and attempt an escape to my room. I thought that if I escaped from Dad's line of sight, it would somehow defuse the situation. Out of sight, out of mind.

Making a quick getaway into my room was not so much a retreat as a flanking maneuver. By changing the war game, I figured it would make my dad desert his attack on my mother and refocus it elsewhere, possibly away from us. My efforts to evade the beating were unsuccessful, however. Dad redirected his attention on me just as I was attempting to close the door to my room.

Bam! Dad blasted open the door with the force of his 230 pounds. With a single swipe of his right arm, he slammed me against the wall. I was stunned from the force of the impact and crumpled to the floor. I was completely helpless, intensely afraid, and slowly losing the will to defend myself. I mustered as much strength as I could. I desperately tried crawling on my hands and knees away from my father. Running for my life was the natural choice.

"Why are you crawling like a coward?" he bellowed, advancing on me like a bullfighter moving in for the kill. "You need to stand up and fight!"

Even a terrified boy was smart enough to realize that any attempt to fight back would only infuriate my father more. Dad's vicious rage would elevate, making the resulting punishment even more brutal. He leaped on top of me and delivered multiple punches to the back of my head, shoulders, and arms. The punches I painfully received were delivered by a man who was blinded by rage and an uncontrollable temper. Most grown men would have difficulty fending off such powerful punches. I frantically tried to protect my head by thrashing my hands and arms, and my mother again tried to halt my Dad's assault. He stood up, turned quickly, and savagely redirected his attack toward Mom, punching her again and again and again. The gruesome sound of a man's fist smacking against a woman's flesh is something I'll never erase from the darkest corners of my memory.

I could no longer stand by and watch my mother being mercilessly beaten, so I rallied my strength, mustered my courage, and stumbled to my feet. In a daze, I jumped on my dad's back, wrapped my arms around his neck, and screamed, "Leave her alone! Stop it! Just leave her alone!"

Dad ripped my arms from around his neck and effortlessly flipped me over his broad shoulders. Then he tossed me against the wall again, as if I were a rag doll. The weakened and now spiritless body of this young boy slumped to the floor. As he stood over me, I looked directly into his eyes and said, "Are you proud of yourself now?" I slowly closed my eyes, turned my head away, and prepared for another volley of punches on my exhausted and defenseless body.

Without any obvious reason, Dad paused, looked at me, and glanced at his battered wife. As quickly as it started, the horror stopped. Dad straightened up, tucked his shirt into his pants, pushed his hair back, and walked to his bedroom as if nothing had happened. Bruised, confused, and exhausted, I felt tightness in my chest, and I began to collect myself. I helped my broken and humiliated mother to her feet. We addressed each other's injuries and hobbled to the bathroom to clean up.

Despite our obvious physical pain and mental turmoil, we had to regroup. In a twisted way, we also had to silently celebrate that the worst was over for now and that we'd live to fight another day. My mother and I both knew that the horror was over for the night, and it was kinder than it might have been. I took some medicine and tried to calm myself, hoping my asthma wouldn't be worse than what we'd just received.

As I lay in bed that night, I tried to analyze the skirmish by looking at the instant replay, just as sports reporters deconstruct a Saturday night boxing match the following morning. Why had the attack stopped as quickly as it had started? I wondered if I'd somehow gained a form of respect from my father by jumping on his back and defending my mom.

This small glimmer of hope opened up another wormhole of speculation. I was confused about why I wanted to gain my dad's respect. Most of my friends didn't have to prove anything to their fathers. They didn't have to wonder why they looked up to their dads with respect and admiration. I wondered why I had to gain *my* dad's respect rather than the other way around.

I slowly fell asleep that night, bruised and battered, thought I knew that the only thing that was really broken was my spirit. I realized I needed to fix my broken spirit and that the only way to do that was by gaining both my father's respect and my own self-respect. It wouldn't be easy. How could it be? There was no logic attached to Dad's reasoning or any method to his madness. With the teachers at school, you could gain respect by studying hard, paying attention, and getting good grades. With the coaches on the football field, respect was earned through blood, sweat, and tears.

However, my dad was the wild card in what most neighbors thought was a cozy, well-adjusted home. We never knew what might set him off. There was no right or wrong thing to say. What inflamed him on Tuesday might not even be a blip on his radar screen come Thursday. On the other side of that dangerous coin, what you'd gotten away with on Wednesday could start World War III come Friday.

It was as if we spoke different languages. Even when we thought we were saying something right, to Dad's ears it sounded all wrong. Unfortunately, there was no translator to clue us in as to what language my father was speaking on any given night. Gradually, I accepted the fact that I should expect more of the same weekend rituals, which were now part of my everyday life. There was no end in sight, no rainbow or pot of gold.

I was right: after that night, the beatings continued like clockwork every Friday or Saturday night for the next few years. They were a regular event, kind of like "Saturday Night at the Fights!" My older brother, Michael, was fortunate to be out with his friends that night, but if he wasn't the target then it was my mother or me—never my little sister, Carol. Only God knows why.

Our house became a battlefield, our living room the scene of countless beatings and terrifying confrontations. We lived in a constant state of fear, walking on eggshells as often as we walked across broken glass from the previous night's brawl.

Everybody in the family reacted differently to the weekend nightmares. My mother made her best attempt to be the peacekeeper, trying to keep Dad placated when nobody else could have risen to such a challenge. Michael was tall, handsome, and slender, with thick, curly black hair and hazel eyes that could look right through you and chill your bones. He was very athletic and was an outstanding first baseman as a southpaw. Michael was more independent than I and had only a few close local friends because he attended a technical school in Providence. He didn't play any high school sports because his school didn't have any teams. Dad's chances of sprouting a pro-athlete with Michael were nonexistent, so Michael was another target of his aggression.

Mike was old enough and smart enough to understand the gravity of the situation. On the weekends, he wisely made it a point to be home as little as possible. I couldn't blame him. I wished I could have done the exact same thing. But then again, who would have been around to help our mother?

Carol, three years younger than I was, would hide in her room and play with her dolls. She sang loudly to block out the sounds of screams, punches, and breaking glass. For whatever reason, my father was kind to Carol, never directing his rage at her, laying a hateful hand on her, or even so much as raising his voice in her direction. She would sit on his lap and, as he brushed her long auburn hair aside, put her head against his shoulder and let him slowly rock her to sleep. How desperately I wanted that affection and attention! However, I was very thankful that my little sister never became another casualty of Dad's silent war.

I often wondered why my mother chose not to leave her husband and search for a better life for herself and her children. Only later, as I grew older, did I realize that we were all victims of our environment and that my mother had nowhere to go. Mother's parents were both deceased, and she knew that by divorcing Dad, she'd face the supposedly shameful consequences that plagued a divorced woman during the 1960s. Fifty years ago, the public viewed a divorcée as promiscuous. The man, of course, faced no such stigma.

Simply walking in the neighborhood for my mother, a churchgoing mother of three, would have been unbearable. At the time there was no Social Security and no battered women's shelters, and she was not about to go back to the housing project to stand in line for the government cheese, powdered milk, and eggs.

Where was a mother with three children, an empty bank account, half an education, deceased parents, and earning sixty-cents-an-hour in a warehouse with no heat or air-conditioning going to go? She was trapped. This was her life, and she made the best of it through her children. She remained silent, never talking about her husband's abusive behavior to anyone. She concealed it for many years.

Her only escape from the daily misery was focusing her thoughts on us. The thought of her children becoming successful brought a smile of self-satisfaction to her face. The smile was a complicated mixture of sadness at her own destitution and pleasure in her children. Mom stood proud, knowing we were the breath of fresh air she so desperately needed.

Chapter 3: *The Equalizer*

Be afraid of no man,
No matter what size.
When trouble threatens, call on me,
For I shall equalize.

~ **Samuel Colt**

There is an indescribable feeling that comes with the never-ending uneasiness of expecting the unexpected. I suppose a psychiatrist is fully capable of making a diagnosis and attaching a medical label to it that ends with "mania" or "phobia." But regardless of the medical jargon, you know it when you feel it begin to smother you, when you've felt it firsthand, and when you've experienced the ugliness of it. Day after day and night after night, there is that queasy feeling of anticipation that sends a chill down your spine and raises the hair on the back of your neck. You're constantly looking over your shoulder and wondering what the trigger is going to be that sets off the explosive night at the fights. The anticipation and fear of being senselessly beaten by your father churn in the pit of your stomach, nauseating you with the foul taste of bile. You don't need a staple or a rubber band to give you a feeling of fullness after only a couple of bites.

Over the next four years, I willed myself into believing that everything would eventually be alright, despite the enormous amount of anger and rage accumulating inside Dad, a ticking bomb. Call it intuition, call it guessing, but something was driving me to hope that Dad would sober up one day and become a loving, caring father and husband. Or he could simply clear out of the apartment and leave us altogether or possibly be struck by lightning. Was my family dreaming that something devastating would happen to Dad, or were we just hoping for anything to happen to make our house a home again? Were we hoping that a mystical or magical event would occur, bringing the daily tension level down several notches and making everyone feel warm, safe, and happy?

Nothing we hoped for, dreamed about, and wished for came to fruition. We had to walk on eggshells around Dad morning, noon, and night. We were skittish like soldiers returning from a combat zone with post-traumatic stress disorder, hitting the floor when a car engine backfired.

School brought me little relief; I still anticipated what might be waiting for me at home later that evening. My ability to concentrate on schoolwork was at best extremely difficult, since I knew there was a high probability that another ugly night awaited me. Wherever I was, I delayed my return home, which seemed to be the safest and wisest choice. Most kids couldn't wait until the bell rang on Friday afternoon; but for me, it was a death knell, signaling the end of safety and plunging me into inescapable danger. The weekend evenings were the worst for whoever happened to be home, bringing forty-eight hours of straight, stark, abject terror.

What would set him off?

What wouldn't? Nobody ever really knew.

Call it self-preservation, maturity, or just plain stupidity, but I realized that survival was important for reasons beyond my own protection. I began to fear that the life of someone in the family was going to be in serious jeopardy. I needed to have a concrete reason, a symbol, that would allow me to rise up and face my father like a man. My search for a reason didn't take very long, nor did I have to look very far. It took just one glance into the kitchen at my mother standing over the sink, cautiously preparing one of her husband's favorite dinners of calf kidneys and tomatoes. My mother and father grew up during the Depression, so this type of meal was common. Whatever meat was on sale fit the Gouins' budget. The sale of the week was very affordable and considered nutritious at the time, but the horrific, subway-like odor made me want to have a clothespin at the ready.

The rancid smell of sautéed cow urine was nauseating. That alone would give anyone more than enough incentive to clear out of the house. Did I eat that yummy, nutritious meal of calf kidneys and stewed tomatoes? Yes. Did I enjoy eating it? No! Nevertheless, that was the menu, and I had no choice.

Although it was neither appetizing nor pleasing to the eye or nose, it pacified the hunger.

Though I'd learned patience, I was also beginning to lose my patience with my father's constant beatings of Mom and his unwarranted slaps on the back of the head. The never-ending barrage of degrading comments regarding my supposedly inept athletic ability, poor posture, or lack of sports knowledge had a cumulative effect. The insults were slowly mounting, and I stored every one in my subconscious. Things were coming to a head, and I contemplated how to put an end to it altogether. I was finally about to stand up to my father's abuse. Still, knowing what I needed to do to get the job done was only scratching the surface of the process leading to my freedom.

I needed a plan, an infallible plan, as if I were preparing to go into battle. I knew there would be only one opportunity. I was extremely confident I was going to complete my mission as planned. I was going to do it correctly the first time, just like the sniper motto, "One shot … one kill!" I was unaware of the significance of this motto at the time, but in only a few years, I would become very familiar with it during my Special Forces tour of duty as a sniper.

I had to identify the enemy. As dreadful as it may sound, the enemy was my father, the source of my flesh and blood. Yes, Dad was the enemy. As Sun Tzu, the great Chinese warrior, wrote in his book *The Art of War* over two thousand years ago and translated by Lionel Giles, "Hence the saying: If you know the enemy and know yourself, you need not fear the result of a hundred battles. If you know yourself but not the enemy, for every victory gained you will also suffer a defeat. If you know neither the enemy nor yourself, you will succumb in every battle."

Well, Dad already knew he had the physical advantage and that I could never match his size and strength. For me to succeed, for my family's suffering to end, there had to be an equalizer. Instinctively, I knew our next-door neighbors, the Smiths and Joneses, wouldn't level the playing field. Rather, it would be two names that were a little more deadly: Smith & Wesson.

I was consumed not so much by visions of grandeur as by real images of rescuing my mother and defending myself with the new equalizer. My mind was filled with these thoughts as I anticipated the usual abusive Friday night. I envisioned the cold steel in my hands and knew that the daily mistreatment of my family would end soon. Determination was my best friend. Failure was not an option. Enough was enough, and things were about to change permanently for every family member.

My decision was set in stone. In the next twenty-four hours, I set the wheels in motion. I spread the word around school that I was looking for a particular item. I told people I normally didn't associate with that I was interested in buying a gun. I especially wanted a handgun that was easy to conceal. I was looking for something I could hold in one hand that would have real live bullets; it only needed to fire once. I wanted to look directly into my father's eyes, ask him if he was alright, and then push the gun against his chest and pull the trigger.

Reactions were mixed. Some people thought I was joking. With the exception of my good friends, most people looked at me as if I were going insane. Others dissociated themselves, not wanting to have anything to do with my plan. Some shrugged their shoulders, others ignored me completely, a few offered suggestions, and some offered names, dates, times, and murky street corners where I might find the item I sought.

Watching old friends run away and new friends greasily smile gave me pause, and I reflected on what I was preparing to do. At times, some friends thought I was having a seizure because I'd wander off, thinking deeply about my plan. Was I setting myself up for failure in the eyes of my mother, my family, or the public? I often considered how the guilt of committing patricide would haunt me endlessly. What kind of son would shoot his own father? It was a gruesome thought, but I felt the end would justify the means.

Despite the fact that the words "son" and "father" had long since lost their true meanings, I remained hopeful that something would change before I pulled the trigger. I rationalized that a normal person wouldn't hesitate to shoot a man beating a defenseless woman to death on the street, so why should the relationship between those two people make any bit of difference?

Though I thought about the consequences of my action, I thought more about the consequences of my inaction. My dad had already ruined my childhood. Would he also destroy my future as a productive man in society? Would he rob me of both my past and my future? Secretly, I envisioned myself spending the rest of my life in prison, coping with dangers hidden behind the concrete, steel, and razor wire. It just didn't make sense. But what in my life ever did? I was willing to throw away my dreams and what little life I had to see the cruelty stop.

Most of my close friends knew I liked guns, but they also knew I'd never owned one. Then, one afternoon as I was getting ready to close my locker at school, another student approached me. He showed me a .32 caliber revolver wrapped in a cotton rag inside a brown paper bag and offered to sell it to me. He gave me a price, I came up with the money, and it was a done deal. Of course, I was extremely nervous. My hands trembled and adrenaline pumped through my body. I'd never done anything as corrupt as this, especially in my own high school. I was definitely not about to look inside the bag right there in the hallway, advertising my new purchase. I just quickly accepted the package, placed it at the bottom of my locker, slammed the steel door shut, and fumbled with the lock. Yes, the deal took place that fast, in a narrow hallway of our small-town high school.

Later that day, I walked home very cautiously, feeling that everyone was looking at me, knowing what I had in that brown paper bag. My self-confidence grew tremendously. I finally had definite hope that all the nightmares were coming to an end. I was no longer defenseless now that I had the equalizer in my back pocket. More importantly, though my mother had no clue, she was no longer defenseless as well. All the way home I leered at this new equalizer and thought about how determined I was to use it. Scratch that: "determined" wasn't exactly the right word for how I felt that day. I was actually looking forward to any excuse to use the shiny, stainless steel, .32 caliber Smith & Wesson military-issue revolver on my prime target, my dad.

My priority that day was to get home from school before Dad. My plan, such as it was, wouldn't work any other way. I had to get there before my father did, and I needed to find a place to hide my new companion. This was no rash act. I planned everything in detail. I needed to conceal the weapon in an inconspicuous place, but it had to be easily accessible in case the situation warranted immediate attention. I would wait for an appropriate time, like a lion silently and stealthily waiting in the tall grass for the opportunity to move in on his prey for the quick kill.

At least I had the main ingredient to the plan.

Now all I needed was an opportunity.

Having arrived home before my dad, I locked myself in my room, eager to hold and feel this finely designed piece of lethal engineering. I cautiously unfolded the soft cloth that enveloped the instrument of death. I polished and caressed it as if it were my best friend.

Like most new friends, we needed to get acquainted. I had read a few books on handguns and followed the steps outlined for a functions check, making sure the weapon wouldn't jam or misfire when the time came to serve its deadly purpose. I practiced loading, unloading, and reloading it, making sure the weapon was ready for the ugliest moment of my life. This was it; the decision was made, and I was ready. Finally, it was going to be over.

At sixteen, the thought of spending the rest of my life in prison seemed unimportant. I was willing to do that for my mother's sake, my own sanity, and my self-respect. It was going to stop. I was going to kill my father, or at least put one, two, or even three lead bullets into him at point-blank range. My love/hate relationship with Dad was on the brink of ending, and I was going to take complete and full responsibility for my actions. I was determined to follow through with stopping him, and absolutely nothing was going to get in my way. Nothing would prevent me from fulfilling my self-assigned assassin's mission.

Everything was ready, and so was I. But then the strangest thing happened at the Gouin residence. Since I had purchased the gun, my father's behavior seemed to have changed for the better. Dad was actually behaving like a real father and a good husband. He was full of compliments, and his demeanor was calm. It was as if he knew what fate was in store for him during the next fit of violence. Dad raised his voice a few times, what we considered minor bouts of rage, a true blessing in this family. For the next few weekends, in fact, there were few problems at all. It was almost a normal home, with a family doing normal things. But a strange, uneasy feeling still loomed over everyone except Dad.

The unusual calmness in the household caused me to question my resolve. Was my dad beginning to realize what he was doing? Was he beginning to change? Did he want to stop drinking? Did he see the pain and heartbreak he'd caused?

I was thoroughly confused, but I was also grateful and happy that the violence appeared to have ended for now. In fact, at one point things were going so well that I forgot I'd hidden the gun in a dresser drawer.

Just as that abusive feeling was starting to drain from my stomach, it came back again with a sudden impact. One Saturday morning in June, an event occurred that I'd never forget. The windows were wide open in the house, and the air was bright, clear, and crisp; everyone was up and ready to do whatever they were going to do for the day. There were no bruises or aches and pains to complain about as I crawled out of bed. There were no headaches or twisted ankles from escaping and evading Dad.

The house was quiet and relatively still as my family of five rose to greet one another for the day. A normal and seemingly peaceful family morning was about to change in an instant. The smell of sizzling bacon and eggs filled the house as Mom prepared breakfast. There was the usual line for the bathroom and the typical squabbling over who got to go first.

Everything seemed as normal as apple pie when it happened just like that. I was walking out of the bathroom, looking down at the floor, when I noticed another pair of feet facing me. They were big feet, not my brother's. I slowly raised my head and glanced up at the massive body blocking my path. Dad was glaring down at me, standing like a stone mountain with his eyes cold and his body rigid.

Looking at him in surprise, I said, "Good morning, Dad!"

Dad had a look on his face that I'd never seen before. It wasn't the glassy-eyed look from two six-packs of beer and a few martinis; it was The Look, that certain look from a parent that every kid knows, the one he immediately understands will bring consequences.

The piercing look penetrated my heart and soul. "Son, today is not going to be your day at the beach!" Dad said loudly. Everything began happening in slow motion. My father's hands were behind his back, and I wondered if he was going to hit me with something. Surely this was not going to happen, not on a Saturday morning when everything had been going so well.

I stood there for a few seconds, expecting to be hit across the head. But for what? I wondered what I'd done this time. The house became silent and all eyes fell on Dad and me. The crackling of the bacon and eggs was the only sound we could hear. As Dad quickly pulled his hands from behind his back, I instinctively ducked. Instead of hitting me, he just looked at me, showed me the gun, and said in a deep, loud, and direct voice, "What is this?"

I was shocked and stunned because there were no slaps, punches, or pepper shakers smashed to the side of my head; he didn't even chase me around the table or call me names. Somehow, though, this was possibly worse. A lump grew in my throat as Dad began to speak to me like a father. He was patient and understanding yet firm in his resolve to reprimand his son.

I was overwhelmed by a feeling of guilt (after all, the gun had been intended for my father); the self-preservation mechanism kicked in again as I tried to save my hide. For the first time in my life, I lied to my dad, but it was probably for a good reason. Lying to him was the absolute worst thing I could do; if he caught one of us in a lie, he rendered a punishment that was extremely swift and painfully severe.

I conjured up a story about how we'd thought the house had been broken and blurted, "I wanted to make sure Mom was alright when you weren't here!"

He calmly looked at me and said, "I don't want any guns in my house, and I will take care of anyone I catch breaking in. Now get the hammer, take this gun outside, and smash it to pieces!"

I did exactly what he ordered me to do. I went outside and began smashing the gun to pieces. Water clouded my eyes as I knelt on the ground, striking the gun harder and harder as if I imagined beating my dad. I saw his face flash in front of me, as if I were sitting on top of him, roles reversed, looking directly into his eyes, and delivering punch after punch. The pieces began to fly everywhere, and my opportunity to fix the problem of a lifetime was now fading into oblivion.

It didn't happen that day. Maybe there was a reason why killing my dad wasn't supposed to happen, or maybe it was simply the dream of killing the habitual nightmares that really died on that day.

Chapter 4: *Fourth and Goal*

A car can massage organs which no masseur can reach. It is the one remedy for the disorders of the great sympathetic nervous system.

~ Jean Cocteau

As was the case with most of the chaos that occurred at home, the gun incident was soon behind us, and life appeared to return to normal. Rather, it was as normal as you could get when you never knew when the next punch was coming or where it was coming from or who was going to be the target for the night. For now, I simply put aside thoughts of what the covert operations world would refer to as "neutralizing" my father.

I thought over the situation and understood that my options were very limited. There had to be some way to stop my father's brutality. Should I slip out of the apartment in the middle of the night and run away, which would ruin my chances for a football career? Should I attempt to convince my mother to leave her husband with what little she had and find a safer place to live? Should we call the police and have him arrested? If this didn't work out, there would be more hell to pay.

The previous path of abuse guided me into understanding that the better part of valor is to avoid confrontations. I thought that focusing my energy on trying to please my father instead of myself was a much healthier idea. My father's blissful contentment was now my major priority, and sports was my method.

My dad's constant abuse was about to lead to an unexpected result. Though I didn't recognize them at the time, I was developing several leadership qualities, including patience, understanding, and unselfishness. An amazing metamorphosis was taking place right before my parents' eyes, but neither one of them could see these changes as they gradually developed. The most obvious trait was mental toughness, my ability to tolerate the most difficult kind of physical and mental stress.

I decided that enduring the abuse was the best and safest way to survive the trauma with as few bruises as possible. I was in survival mode, dedicated to making my father proud and avoiding more ill-fated weekends. It was a symbiotic relationship. The more attention I received from the media regarding my athletic ability, the more content and docile my dad became on the weekends.

As a young athlete, I considered it necessary to push my mental toughness to the limit. Pleasing my father became a mission, an obsession. I excelled in athletics, and, in turn, I gained the attention of the local media and pleased my father. No matter how difficult the task, I always tried to be the best at anything I attempted. Just being good or above average was substandard for me; I had to be the best, always the best, at whatever I did. Other kids had the luxury of dropping out of an activity when things got too hard or going inside when it got too hot or cold. That sort of behavior and that kind of thinking weren't in my realm of possibility. My positive attitude, determination, and dedication to athletics directed me to put my head and eyes forward, and I pushed myself harder and harder. I was the driving force of my family's peace of mind on the weekends.

Never saying "no" or "I quit" became my hallmark and my personal calling card; these words were simply not in my vocabulary. I absolutely could not allow those ludicrous, self-destructive words to enter my life, although there were many times when I was tempted to shout them from the highest rooftop or scream them from the peak of a mountain. Placing my head in my hands or between my knees to cry was not an option. To my dad, this would have been the epitome of insults: weakness! "No, my son," he'd say. "You will not act like a little quitter or a sissy boy!"

In my dad's family, it was virtually unheard of to quit anything, especially a sport. He would simply not hear of it. Worse still, he made sure everyone else heard about it if I *attempted* to break ranks and actually quit something. The resulting combination of embarrassing social consequences and verbal abuse motivated me to concentrate all my efforts on doing extremely well in athletics. Unfortunately, academics were secondary because of my dad's level of education. This narrowed my thinking. I believed that if you had the raw talent, everything else would fall into place.

For some kids, getting into college was their reason for ramping up social, academic, and extracurricular activities; others were set on meeting chicks or hanging out with fellow fraternity brothers. For me, getting into college was a way to the NFL, keeping my dad happy and literally off my back and the rest of the family's as well.

Many athletes, either professional or amateur, dedicate games to their mothers. What are the first words most athletes say when they're on the sidelines and the television camera pans past them? "Hi, Mom!" For those players, it's a tribute, a sign of gratitude, and a form of acknowledgement for their fortunate upbringing. I dedicated all my games to my mother, but my dedication was for an entirely different reason. I was determined to beat the snot out of the guy in front of me every play and every game. Was there a direct correlation between the number of games when I had a field day with my opponent and a decrease in the number of beatings my mother received at home? To me, this was a fair trade-off, but I'm sure it didn't seem this way to the guy who played directly across that line from me.

No matter what, I always tried to make the best of my athletic opportunities. For instance, I participated in every sport I had time for; indoor and outdoor track, including throwing the shot put, discus, and javelin, was the perfect way to improve my strength, speed, and power. I also weight-lifted to prepare for the next football season. Likewise, basketball improved my coordination, endurance, and agility for track. On and on it went, one season spilling over into the next and that season spilling over into another. These athletic activities consumed nearly all of my free time. I wouldn't allow any energy to be wasted or a drop of sweat to be spilled in vain; there had to be a reaction for an action. My ultimate goal was still pro football; I was a boy who wanted it all. But my short-term goals were keeping Mom safe—and Dad happy.

I eventually began to think that I was designed for sports as if I were a human athletic machine, a thoroughbred, never satisfied, obsessed to the point where I could never get enough physical activity. While other kids thought about an event beforehand, considering the consequences of doing this or their motivation for doing that, I just went out and did it. I kept my reasons to myself, a secret only known to my family. My body was the only conscience I had, and I was going to put every ounce of character into it that I possibly could to become a highly competitive and successful athlete.

I exercised, lifted, and pumped until my muscles could take no more, and then I would collapse from fatigue and rest until I could pump some more. Downtime was for rest and repairing muscles, tendons, ligaments, bumps, and bruises, not for soul searching or getting in touch with my inner child. I had little time for childish nonsense; I was goal-oriented and sometimes felt I didn't quite fit in with my high school peers at parties and gatherings.

Goals; it was all about my goals. My long-term goal was to stay healthy, alive, and physically fit; avoid devastating injuries; and catch the eye of a university football recruiter. My short-term goal was to participate in any and every sporting event that was available. In addition to excelling as an individual in the sports of my choice, I knew I needed to prove myself as a leader, which wasn't as easy as it sounded.

Life at home had sapped my self-confidence, and I struggled with meeting girlfriends and hanging out with other athletes. I had problems in school, where I was afraid to speak up. I feared embarrassing myself by giving a wrong answer when the teacher asked a question. I doubted myself in just about everything except sports, which were my only salvation. On the playing field, my confidence came naturally. My thinking was on automatic pilot, and all I really needed to do was make the human machine do what I wanted it to do.

Move is exactly what I did. If the track coach said he needed someone for the 100-yard, 220-yard, or even the 440-yard dash, I'd volunteer without hesitation and do the best I could to win. My main events in track were the shot put, javelin, and discus; on occasion, I'd even high jump if the coach needed me to. I had to be the best at something to achieve my own self-respect and, by association, gain my father's as well, which was not going to be any small feat.

Football season neared. Thanks to my tireless training and competition in other sports, I was well prepared physically and mentally. Nothing was going to get in the way of my dominance and success on the football field. My mental toughness wouldn't even allow the asthma attacks. I kept them a secret, wheezing and quietly tolerating the misery through entire games and practices.

The fact that I had difficulty breathing was becoming harder and harder to ignore, but that didn't mean I'd allow for any cracks in the armor I'd worked so hard to build and polish over the past few years. Of course, Superman's demise was kryptonite, and even my body could withstand only so much abuse and punishment. Twice I needed to go to the emergency room for injections for a severe attack. Again, I didn't tell anyone, not a soul. I learned to keep secrets as a direct result of my experience with asthma. My secrets didn't matter if they were about anything I was very good at doing all too well.

Of course, the asthma attacks were a little easier to keep secret than the outer ills that started creeping up as the school year dragged on. Even the magic of youth cannot prevent an injury when the human body is pushed to its limits of endurance. At last, slowly developing chronic pain in my left knee was slowing me down on the field. A serious injury would be disastrous and ruin any chances for a collegiate or professional career.

Amazingly, my father was the first to point out my newly discovered problem with my knee. He'd noticed that I was limping after practices and through most of the games. Wrapping the knee and getting cortisone shots gave me some temporary relief, but the inevitable was rapidly approaching. Missing a game was unacceptable, unconscionable, especially when the team counted on me to play both ways on offense and defense.

Ills and pills and aches and pains aside, I was having a great junior year as a starter for the football team. It was such a strange time for me as I bridged the worlds of school and home. In the house, I was just another punching bag, expecting another punch; but at school, I was a legendary football star and everybody's hero. I couldn't imagine that any of the students who stepped aside for me in the halls suspected that I, too, cringed in my father's wake. We must all answer to a higher power, someone, somewhere, and sometime.

Even so, all my hard work on the playing field was finally beginning to pay off, not only with college scouts but at school as well. Students would recognize me on Monday morning after cheering for me on the previous Saturday morning. I tried to keep a level head and knew I needed to keep it all in perspective. Maybe it was the constant threat of pain at home that kept me modestly humble in school.

Whatever the reason, I decided to test my newly discovered notoriety out on my dad. I waited for the perfect moment, when he wasn't excessively drinking and after I'd had a fantastic game. My dad had noticed the large amount attention I was getting from the local media, the local sports bars, and my friends. So I figured this would be an opportune time to test my newfound popularity with my father.

The subject of the All-state football team came up when a few of my father's fellow football officials had gathered after one of my games. As they sat around the table drinking beer, I overheard them mention my name. One of the officials said, "Jack, I think your son has a good chance of making the All-state high school football team as a junior."

My father replied, "Come on, you guys! You know that making the All-state team as a junior is nearly impossible."

I walked over to the kitchen table and jumped on the opportunity to put my dad in a precarious position. I knew I could force him to make a commitment in front of his friends. I hesitated at first, mindful of the potential repercussions that I'd suffer if my plan backfired. I took a deep breath and blurted out, "Dad, if I make All-state as a junior, will you buy me a car?"

The room fell silent. My dad's friends swiftly turned their eyes to him, waiting for an answer. He paused for a second. I could tell by the expression on his face that I'd made a move that could cost me a serious blow. But then he replied, "If you make All-state as a junior, I will buy you a car."

I knew he'd never go back on his word now that he'd given it in front of his friends. I also knew there might be some painful consequences since I'd put him in such an awkward situation in the first place. I was not disappointed. As his friends left the apartment one by one, my father looked at me and said, "You put me in a very bad and embarrassing position." I decided not to reply; I didn't want to aggravate the situation. I felt it was in my best interest that I never bring up the subject again for the rest of the year.

The season went extremely well for me, despite my painful left knee. Dad had been watching me limp after every game and decided to schedule an appointment with an orthopedic surgeon. The doctor examined my knee and determined that my problem was a childhood ailment called Osgood Schlatter's disease. It generally struck boys between the ages of ten and sixteen, affecting the front of the knee and the ligaments attaching the kneecap. He recommended that I have surgery at the end of the season to eliminate the constant, excruciating pain. I wondered whether the surgery would bring the end of my very young career or enhance it. My future as an athlete depended on the hands of the surgeon, the health of my body, and the grace of God.

As it turned out, several weeks after the season finished, I had the surgery. While recovering at home on a cold December day and reading the state's most popular Sunday newspaper, I got quite a start. There on the cover of the sports section was my picture, along with ten other players.

Being awarded a position on the All-state football team as a junior was quite an honor, and it took me completely by surprise. All my hard work had finally paid off. I did it, and I was proud. I also knew my dad was just as proud, but he had a debt to pay, a promise to keep, and I was not about to hound him for the reward. I was not about to throw my accomplishment in his face. I knew better than to stir up the hornet's nest.

I maintained my silence about the car and thought my father had forgotten all about our bet. I left the subject alone. As spring came and went, so did the thought of a car. I wasn't disappointed and hand no resentment toward my father; I just assumed it was a money issue. I was determined to stay positive, keep my goals in sight, and make All-state as a senior. My head and eyes were looking forward.

As I came home from school late one Friday afternoon, I thought about the promise my father had made to me in front of his friends and how that promise hadn't come to fruition. I opened the door of the apartment, and there, boldly standing directly in the middle of the living room, was my dad. A cold chill ran through my body as he greeted me with his deep, powerful voice. "Where have you been? I've been waiting for you all afternoon!" I felt my stomach turn; I thought something bad was about to happen, and, of course, I was usually right in the middle of the action.

I'd anticipated the worst and noticed my dad's hands tucked behind his back. I instantly flashed back to the gun incident and expected the inevitable. I didn't know what I'd done this time and was totally disgusted by my nervous apprehension. Nevertheless, I could see my mother standing behind my dad with a most unusual smile, which confused me. As Dad brought his hands forward, they appeared to move in slow motion. I waited for the dreaded slap in the face or the back of the head.

What did I do this time? I thought to myself. Dad raised his right hand over his head and dangled a set of keys. I still wasn't sure what was going on. Then he said, "It's yours. Go take a look outside."

Without even grabbing the keys, I went outside, and there was a white two-door 1958 Chevy Bellaire. I looked at my dad and said one word: "Mine?"

He responded, "Yes, it's yours. I'm keeping my promise to you, the all-state deal we made several months ago."

I was ecstatic and could barely believe my eyes. "It's mine, all mine!" I said. I wondered how my father could afford to give his son a car. Of course, I knew the money came from him officiating football games and gambling at the club. He was keeping his promise, but there was one condition. In a commanding voice, he said, "You have to make all-state again as a senior if you want to keep the car." Rather than being offended, I agreed on the spot. After all, I'd made All-state once, and I was confident that I was going to do it again, providing I didn't get injured. I had no problem committing myself at this point.

My senior athletic year was better than my junior year. It seemed I could do no wrong. College scouts came to every football game, basketball game, and even track meet! I received dozens and dozens of recruitment letters from many different schools all over the country. I had so many options that I wasn't sure where to begin. I didn't know where I wanted to go to college. Should I be a big fish in a small pond or a small fish in the ocean? I was about to move up one notch in the hierarchy of football players, and I knew I was just one level below the pros. My goals were slowly taking shape and beginning to come to life!

I asked Dad to meet some coaches with me after a game, and he was thrilled. When the coaches came to our house that night, they offered me a full four-year athletic scholarship. They talked about the details and told my dad that he should be proud of me and that the college coaches expected big things from this aspiring young man. I knew that coach had hit pay dirt with my father. Dad was prouder than a peacock.

I had some difficult choices to make. After several months of thinking things over, I finally decided to attend a local university so Mom and Dad could have the opportunity to watch me play. I knew that if I went to Kentucky or Florida, two schools that aggressively recruited me, the chances of my parents watching me play were going to be slim.

Therefore, I concluded that being a big fish in a small pond was much better than being a small fish in the big ocean. It was a difficult decision and one I would not regret. I wanted my father to watch his son become successful. More importantly, I wanted my deserving mother to enjoy watching one of her sons succeed at something so important in his life.

Chapter 5: *September 1974*

You can encounter many defeats, but you must not be defeated.

~ Maya Angelou

Many college freshmen experience a rocky transition as they move from being high school seniors to being the new kids on the block, but this wasn't the case for me. The realization set in early that I was no longer going to be a big fish in a small pond but was about to be that small fish in the ocean and enter the aggressively competitive world of college football. Obsessively staying active and fit, I prepared myself mentally and physically for the demanding challenges that awaited me as a college athlete. My desire to stand out as a winning athlete and become successful steamrolled me straight into the end of summer and directly into triple-session football practices.

I didn't break; I rolled like a boxer turning his head with punch after punch. I woke up each morning and tackled the day as a new challenge, working out harder and becoming stronger while never losing sight of my ultimate goal, the NFL.

Growing up in an abusive household taught me that determination was what I needed to leave behind a world of fear, but physical and emotional strength was required to make it happen. My mother tried her best to instill politeness, manners, and solid emotional and social values in her children, but these lessons were hard to hear over Dad's commanding voice and powerful disciplinarian hands. I came away from my youth knowing exactly what was going to work for me and what was not. I learned the hard way that the combination of strength and intelligence was a powerful force to be reckoned with; weakness and stupidity took a backseat to everything else.

My first year as a college athlete earned me little recognition in the community, but the coaching staff noted the outstanding talent and drive of this young freshman. My physical stature was still too small at six foot three, 220 pounds, and I needed to bulk up in order to compete in my position as an offensive tackle against the much larger and more experienced senior players. I was determined not to let my size inhibit my chances of getting a starting position.

Despite having a great freshman football season, I was failing to perform well academically; I refused to realize the importance of this until later. I had the letters "NFL" branded in my mind, and I was determined that nothing would stop me from achieving my dream. Like many players, I didn't make much of an effort at the academic portion of my college career. I was confident that I wouldn't need an education after making it to the NFL because of the great bonuses and salaries that lead to a comfortable, affluent life. My thinking was obscured by my determination and obsession to play pro football, which led me to make a serious mistake in my life: neglecting my education. This would come back to haunt me in the future.

As my freshman transition came to a rapid close, a long, hard road to self-discovery lay ahead with new and exciting challenges. Just as the hard-won lessons of my youth paid off in high school, I was beginning to reap the benefits of being a student-athlete at a university. I continued to dream and began to see a bright, successful future in front of me. My life was gradually falling into place exactly as I'd planned, and my goal was getting closer. Thanks to my hard work, the path was beginning to clear and a career in professional football was imminent. Sure, I was probably never going to be another Dick Butkus, one of pro football's hardest-hitting players, but I was positive I was going to get there just the same. All I needed now was a little luck along with my hard work, and the rest would fall into place. I was so optimistic that I could feel the beat of success throbbing deep within my heart.

Over the next three years, I practiced hard, worked out religiously, and ate healthy, which I enjoyed tremendously. I gave football my greatest effort, turning everything over to my future and taking little for myself in the near-term. I dedicated 100 percent to every play. I felt like it was an instant replay of high school: making new friends, being recognized as a formidable player by my teammates, receiving praise from the coaching staff, and rapidly becoming a BMOC (big man on campus). My mother had to start filling another scrapbook with all my new pictures and news clippings. Meanwhile, her handsome, jock son was being invited to all the college parties and socials.

I accepted the adulation and special treatment I was getting in college the same way I accepted it in high school, with mild amusement and occasional indifference. I partied like most of my friends but managed to avoid becoming a complete party animal, and, so far, it was paying off where it mattered most: on the playing field.

My college and professional football career were apparently on a golden path to success. I had the heart, probably the most essential component required to play good, hard, in-your-face football; and being smart, strong, fast, and fearless made my fellow teammates, coaches, and fans take notice. I was considered the "whole ball of wax" by most college coaching and recruiting standards. I simply needed some shaping, molding, and grooming to become a great player for the NFL. The largest newspaper in the state also observed my promise by giving me the nickname "the Man Mountain of Steel." Word spread via the news media and traveled fast through the local community, especially among my hometown followers. Several professional scouts and recruiters took an interest in my athletic capabilities and potential as a professional prospect. There was a very real possibility that I was a candidate for the upcoming NFL draft. I was hopeful but also realistic that the selection would occur in the later rounds, if at all.

Once again, fate reared her head just as I was ramping up to accept my rightful spot in the elite world of professional sports. Unbeknownst to me, my so-called promising football career was coming to a rapid and certain close. I had just started a great senior season. During the second game of the season, with every seat in the small stadium filled on a sunny autumn morning, I received a devastating injury in the third quarter on a punt.

My right knee exploded with excruciating pain when another player hit me from the left side. I'd made one of the most elementary and fundamental mistakes in football: I locked my knee and planted my foot firmly on the ground as the other player was blocking me from the left side at shoulder level. You never lock your knees, never! You keep your legs moving and always driving. How could I have let this happen? What was I thinking?

As an opposing player blocked me and drove directly through my upper body, the powerful force of the impact caused my right knee to buckle inward and collapse on itself. There was no loud snap like my father's career-ending injury, and the immediate silence drowned out the roar of the fans. As I lay on the field in pain, with the trainer working on my knee, I saw all my due diligence, training, and dedication flash before my eyes. In an ironic twist of fate on that cold October morning, my football career was going to end, just as my dad's had.

My father attended most of the games and, unfortunately, was in the stands that day, watching his son tumble to the ground in pain. Did my dad relive his own injury that day as he hoped and prayed that it was something minor and that I'd be fine for the next game? Did his visions of my promising NFL career go out the window, along with his image of himself as a proud father?

The injury was devastating, with the dreadful signs of what the industry pros call the "unhappy triad": a torn cartilage and two torn ligaments. Specifically, it was the medial collateral ligament, medial meniscus, and anterior cruciate ligament. I didn't need to see the trainers' somber faces to know that this type of injury was usually terminal; at least it was during the 1970s, before the use of arthroscopy.

My career and training from that moment on were now focused solely on rehabilitation. I had several visits with orthopedic physicians and hours and hours of physical therapy, but all this would prove hopeful at best and only minimally promising at worst. I had seen the results of similar surgeries on other teammates and decided not to have surgery at this point. Unwilling and unable to give up my dream, I simply shifted my focus. Prior to the mishap, all my energy had been put toward winning games; now it was being put toward staying alive and healthy in the cutthroat world of collegiate football and the NFL.

I tried not to let the depressing locker room gossip and general disinterest bother me, but it wasn't easy, especially when the pro scouts came by to talk with some of the team's other pro prospects. There was no longer any noticeable interest in me whatsoever. It was as if I'd suddenly become invisible.

After missing the next three games because of rehab, I felt I was strong and healthy enough to play and suited up for a mid-season game. Despite the rehab, strengthening exercises, taping, and brace, my knee continued to pop out painfully during every game and practice. After another disappointing, physically painful game, my naiveté began to show, and I decided I needed to find out why the scouts and recruiters no longer displayed any interest in me. Of course, I knew the reason perfectly well, but I needed to hear it for myself. With an ice pack wrapped around my knee, I approached one of recruiters in the training room, one with whom I was familiar from an earlier visit. This scout was a recruiter for several professional teams, including the Dallas Cowboys, New York Giants, and Oakland Raiders. I asked him, "Why haven't I heard from any of the teams regarding the draft?"

The scout looked at the floor, considering his words. Then he raised his head and said cockily, "Son, you aren't *going* to hear anything from any team."

My stomach dropped. "Why not?" I said. "I can still complete a forty-yard dash in 4.7 seconds with an injured knee."

The scout seemed annoyed with my frustration. He slowly leaned over and said in a low southern drawl, "Lookie here, son. You're not going to hear anything. You got hurt, that's all there is to it. I can find twenty players just as *big* as you, just as *fast* as you, and just as *strong* as you who played at bigger schools—and they don't have any injuries." The scout gave me an insulting smirk, patted me on the shoulder, and wished me luck.

The realization hit me like a ton of bricks. There would be no NFL for me. My lifelong dream, to which I'd committed hard work, sacrifice, and pain, was beginning to fade. Despite my intelligence, I'd put minimal effort into academics over the last three years, a choice that was about to come back and haunt me. I'd wanted to play pro football; and for me, like most college athletes, collegiate football was a way to get there.

The sudden awareness of my fate would have been easier to take if I hadn't attached family members to so many of my own dreams. All that I'd planned to do for my siblings was now impossible. Worst of all, the dream house I'd imagined for my mother was never going to appear.

As the season ended and the new semester started, I eagerly awaited the results of the NFL draft. I wasn't sure who I was fooling. Was it my family, my friends, or myself? The NFL draft came and went, and I was left alone as though I were the last one standing in musical chairs. Imagining I still had a chance to make a team wasn't entirely wishful thinking, since there were many players with injuries in the NFL. Just when I thought all hope was lost, I received a call from a team, probably the worst team in NFL history in the mid 1970s. The New England Patriots were interested in having me sign a free agent contract and try out for the team. Obviously, I jumped at the opportunity to sign the contract and asked my dad to join me for the signing. I knew it would make my father proud, and dad was in his glory. His son was about to make it to the NFL! I was so excited that I was already making plans to attend all the practice sessions at Foxboro Stadium.

I jumped in my father's car, and together we drove to the stadium, approximately thirty minutes from our home in Rhode Island. I couldn't sit still. We barely spoke a word during the drive. As we pulled up to the stadium, I gasped, thinking that today was the day I would enter the world of professional football.

We walked to the administrative part of the stadium and found the recruiter who prepared the contract for me to sign. My dad was extremely quiet that morning; he, too, was awestruck by what we were about to do. The recruiter greeted us in a room filled with New England Patriots memorabilia; my heart began to race, and my palms turned sweaty. This was it, the biggest day of my life. In front of me was a contract that allowed me the opportunity to make the team.

The recruiter unfolded the blue fourteen-inch document on the team letterhead and carefully reviewed the contract details. He handed me a pen and asked me to initial the paragraphs as he detailed each one. Dad proudly looked on as my hands shook with excitement. I was signing a three-year contract with a professional football team. My dream was coming true.

To wrap things up, the recruiter finished discussing his expectations of me, the team requirements, and the date to report to camp. He handed me a playbook with an exercise program and said he'd see me in May.

Maybe my dreams weren't over after all—or so I thought.

I worked out and read all the plays from the team playbook. I was determined to be physically and mentally prepared to play pro football. The day I reported to the pre-season training camp, my excitement grew. It felt less like a dream come true and more like a prophecy fulfilled. I felt deep down inside that I was built and designed for this; it was my destiny.

This was just how it was supposed to be.

I reported exactly at the weight they required, 228 pounds, for the weak-side linebacker position, and I thought I was physically ready. However, there were two things going against me before I even set foot on the practice field. First, I'd never played linebacker; and second, my devastating injuries weakened my agility and lateral movement. During the practice sessions, my knee repeatedly gave out. A few plays later, I noticed the coaches on the sidelines and could tell they were talking about me—and what they were saying didn't appear the least bit positive.

During one specific play, I had pass coverage on a well-known wide receiver. This receiver outclassed me with some hip fakes and moves that would shock Fred Astaire. I could barely keep up with him, tripping, falling, and, of course, watching from the ground as the receiver dashed into the end zone. I'd eaten an embarrassing face full of turf. As the receiver ran back to the huddle, he passed me and patted me on the rear, saying in a cocky tone of voice, "Nice try, rookie!" A cold chill streaked through my body.

During the scrimmages, my job on certain plays was to prevent the running back from getting to the outside of the line and me. On the offensive line, there are guards who are about six foot five and close to three hundred pounds pulling in front of the back and clearing the way for him to get past the defenders. It's scary to see two huge men running at full speed around the offensive corner like raging bulls, knowing you're their red cape.

I continued to hold my own, despite the fact that my knee prevented me from performing the way I needed to in order to make the team. Dad watched from the stands every day during the practices, taking photos and making mental notes to discuss with me later that evening. Dad's comments included, "You look lost out there, like you don't know what you're doing." Of course, this was an unfamiliar position for me to be in. I was doing my best, but it wasn't good enough.

A couple of days later, I received the dreaded letter of termination. I held my head up, proud that I did my best, as I emptied my locker, shook hands with some other players, packed up, and headed home. Surprisingly, I found a letter waiting for me from another team. An expansion team, the Cincinnati Bengals, had requested that I report to camp and try out for a linebacker position on the team. However, I knew better than to tempt fate twice. The Patriots had been a losing team since their inception, and an expansion team was asking me if I wanted to try out. It was time to start looking for a different line of work.

My dream was over, my NFL fantasies dashed. It was the first time I'd ever considered quitting anything, especially football. In my heart, I knew it was the beginning of the end. It was time for me to make a change in my life and find a new direction. At one time or another, every person realizes that it's time for a change. You can rationalize the change, believing you're not actually quitting but just making a change for the better. Quitting seemed so permanent; but I decided it was time to make a life change. I never responded to the new team. I felt like I'd lost my best friend. I looked in the mirror and had a long, serious talk with myself. I added everything up, and it just didn't make sense anymore. I was just cut from a last-place team, and an expansion team that had never played a game in the NFL wanted me to try out. I needed to explore an alternative career path, though I wasn't sure what that looked like yet. I had to deal with deep-seated disappointment and bitterness. I knew I'd never walk on a football field again as a player or a coach.

In the wake of such unfortunate events, I decided to do some soul searching and change direction. Of course, I had no idea what my new career might be, nor did I have any motivation to find it. But the decision to look for another career, without knowing what I really wanted to be when I grew up, seems indicative of my state of mind at the time.

For so long, football had been *the* career. The best part was that I was already there, doing it, living the dream. The demanding practices, the exciting games, and even the hours of rehab seemed like on-the-job training. Now that my job was gone, why did I continue to train? I'd only gone to school to play football, so what was the use? Stumbling from class to class and hearing my peers chatter about this term paper or that final exam just made me feel like an imposter. What was I still doing there, a failing student at best?

I returned home with a heavy heart and no place to live other than with my parents. My dad was more than disappointed and handled it in his usual demeaning style. He started right in with his insults and the negative comments I'd grown up with: "You didn't try hard enough! You could have made it! What was wrong with you? You looked like you didn't know what was going on out there on the field!" Whether my father's comments were meant to be demeaning or simply motivational, I'll never know.

I listened to his humiliating remarks day after day for months on end. What else could I do? I was under his roof again, with no money and no job. I was a typical loser, with nowhere to go and nowhere to be and in no great hurry to get where I already was. My dad's shouts and putdowns didn't even seem to be all that bad. I was twenty years old, and the worst part for me was that I was finally starting to believe my dad's remarks.

I knew I needed to find some kind of work, so I looked for a job at a popular nightclub. That one visit to the nightclub was about to change everything for me forever. My world was about to spin on its axis and leave me standing 180 degrees from any place I'd ever been. I started my quest for a career with no hope and no future; I'd end it with just enough of both to save my life.

I dreaded the thought of spending another evening at home, listening to my father play Dr. Phil's evil twin, so I began to consider my options. My résumé up to this point wasn't exactly stellar. Take off football and all that remained was a below-average student with exclusively physical extracurricular activities.

After spending my entire lifetime pursuing football, I had nothing to show for it but a wall full of trophies and hundreds of newspaper clippings. I had no part-time job, no typing skills, not even a local lemonade stand or paper route. I'd worked part-time in a supper club one summer and thought nightclubs might be a logical choice. What other choice did a man like me have other than to utilize my physical talents?

After asking the manager of one nightclub for a job as a bouncer and getting immediately turned away, I reached the lowest point in my life. I couldn't even be hired as a bouncer. The slap in the face came hard and swift, bringing me to my broken knees. The simple truth was that I'd been a dumbass. How ignorant it was to completely waste a college education that I could have gotten for free for playing football! I was about to pay the price for not taking advantage of that golden opportunity.

If only I'd realized that actually being hired for a job would speed my descent in an uncontrollable downward spiral. I approached the manager of another nightclub, a man named Anthony, who was about my age and clearly living an enviable lifestyle. I asked him if there were any openings for a bouncer, a doorman, or a bar tender. As I looked around the bar, he said casually, "No, but you're welcome to stay and have a few drinks on me." That was the extent of the conversation; the grueling job interview ended with a handshake and a free beer.

With nothing better to do and an old man at home who'd surely start a fight when I came through the door empty-handed, I took the manager up on his offer and hung around at the bar for a while, drinking a few beers.

I turned green with envy as I watched Anthony, wondering how he'd made his way to his current position. I sat there alone, looking around the bar and thinking about how broke I was and how I'd struggled for years trying to make my dream come true. How was it possible that I could have been so close to reaching my dream? It had been right around the corner, but now I knew it was never going to happen. The thought of all that hard work, enthusiasm, and devotion made me cringe.

However, my perception of what appeared to be a better way of life clouded my judgment. I believed it was glamorous to socialize with all kinds of people in the nightclub, meet beautiful women, drive fancy cars, and make lots of money—or at least pretend to be rich.

After I spent my last few dollars on a beer and talked to a few of the bouncers in the club, I decided I wanted to call it a night. I was eager to thank Anthony for his hospitality and looked around the club. I couldn't help but notice some commotion occurring outside the club's front door. There in the middle of a group of shouting men stood Anthony with a bouncer, and they were clearly outnumbered. Only seconds after I noticed that Anthony was in a jam, one of the men suddenly attacked him, knocking him to the ground. I was compelled to do whatever I could to help him avoid a serious beating.

I ran down a small flight of wooden stairs, my footsteps sounding like a rumbling tank, and burst out the door. I saw the men kick and throw punch after punch at Anthony's face, and I instinctively began to help fend them off. I just couldn't stand by and not help; it wasn't in my nature. Here at last was an opportunity in disguise where I could be of service. I knew I was strong and powerful, and I'd built up so much anger inside me that I was just waiting to explode on someone or something.

I forced my way through the small crowd of cheering spectators and zoomed in on the first attacker, getting him in a chokehold. My quick thinking allowed Anthony an opportunity to defend himself. The chokehold I had around the first man was beginning to work; the man slowly stopped thrashing and trying to fight back. I released the chokehold, grabbed the man by his collar, and, with my left hand, turned him around so we were face to face. As the man continued to struggle, I released a barrage of punches directly onto the side of the man's head, causing him to fall to the ground. It was a scene right out of a hockey game, when a player is holding onto another player's jersey, throwing punches in the middle of a fight on the ice.

I knew the man wouldn't be getting up anytime soon, so I zoomed right over to help Anthony. At this point, I was in a rage, blinded by everything else going on around me and totally focused on what I needed to do. I was in the zone. I vice-gripped the second guy by the shirt collar and delivered another vicious beating; blood splattered over my clothes. This man knew he'd had enough and eventually was able to free himself by squirming away, not by breaking away from my grip but by tearing his shirt apart and leaving me with a souvenir piece of silk.

The beaten man's friend slowly helped him to his feet. With their clothes tattered and faces bruised, they wearily made it out to the street and their car. For an instant, I stood there staring at the piece of the man's shirt I clutched in my hand. I flashed back to my childhood, when my dad had grasped my arm during his fits of rage. However, there was a huge difference between the two types of beatings. One was man-to-man, and the other was man-to-child.

A police car, its blue lights flashing, screeched to a halt outside the club. The officers immediately began to disperse who was left of the onlookers. I put out my hand to help Anthony to his feet. Brushing the dirt off his back, I asked him, "Are you okay?"

"I'm okay. Thanks for your help!" He wiped some blood off his lip. Then he looked me right in the eye, shook my hand, and said with a painful smile, "You're hired, and you can start tonight!"

It was great news. I'd always had an interest in owning or managing a restaurant or a nightclub, and this was a perfect opportunity to gain some experience in the business. My appreciation for the restaurant business started while I was a salad boy, making salads at a local Italian restaurant. I watched intently as the chef prepared his own special blend of herbs and spices for Italian-style chicken with baked ziti. I knew it wasn't much of an art, but I was taught how to use a kitchen knife and put a great salad together. The job only lasted for a summer because working on weekends interfered with my participation in high school athletics. But the part-time job was enough to arouse my curiosity about the restaurant or nightclub business.

Little did I realize that that night was going to be the beginning of an adventure that would nearly cost me my life, literally and figuratively. It turned out that Anthony (not his real name) was the son of a notorious underworld figure. Over the next year, we'd become almost inseparable as friends and co-workers.

Anthony was the archetypal "Goodfella." He had Italian features; was tall, dark, and handsome; and, what's more, his magnetic personality made him very attractive to women. He exuded danger with every step. Who he was, what he did, whom he was connected to—you couldn't separate the man from the myth. Women were probably infatuated more with his lifestyle and his position as club owner than with his charismatic personality. Anthony was a magnet for all kinds of things, women as well as fortune, and he always had an eye open for an opportunity to make money.

It didn't take long for us to become inseparable; in fact, we bonded the very first night we met. Wherever Anthony was, I was right there with him, like a pit bull. Part bouncer, part bodyguard, part lackey, part friend, wherever you found Anthony, you inevitably found me. I was soon to lead the life of a wise guy. Notoriety, money, women, clothes, luxury, and sports cars were just rolling in; I was just twenty years old, and I couldn't resist the powerful pull into this shady world. But hidden behind the glamour, I realized that I'd obtained a false sense of importance and lost my real life priorities.

It wasn't hard to see where my trouble came from. I had gone from zero to sixty in a single bar fight. I really wasn't any different from the thousands of other athletes in America. My unfortunate injury curtailed my chance at a pro football career. I was your typical nobody, with half an education, when things changed seemingly overnight. I'd gained respect, although at that point I didn't realize it was pseudo-respect, from new friends and foes alike. Without ever suiting up or buttoning a chinstrap on a football helmet, I'd regained my sense of self-worth and achieved the level of fame and celebrity I'd missed by being out of the spotlight. Suddenly, people I didn't know would come up to me just to pay their respects with a handshake or a cocktail, the ultimate sign of respect in a bar. How could I have fallen for such trivial signs of respect? At the time, it seemed important, I felt important, and I was enjoying the lifestyle.

Gradually, I was considered a smalltime goon by my college football friends, who were making a good living with their completed education. I was shaking people down, beating people up, dabbling in all kinds of cut-rate intimidation with drive-by shootings into homes, and being paid handsomely to do it. If Anthony wanted someone or something taken care of, it was done, no questions asked. If he wanted me to intimidate someone, then it was done. (I just thanked God that Anthony never asked me to kill anyone; that's where I would have drawn the line.)

I was intimidating with my size, strength, and viciousness, yet I had a docile demeanor. People often commented on how ruthless I could be, but I separated the real me from the work me. I was a good guy; my job entailed doing bad things sometimes. What was the big deal? It was just a job.

Although it wasn't obvious to me at the time, I was the mirror image of my dad, mimicking the beatings that occurred every Friday and Saturday night in my youth. The only difference was that I was beating up strangers for money; the violence wasn't directed at family members or loved ones, and it never happened at home, only at the club. It was almost as if I had a split personality. At the club, I was one guy, but at home, I was completely different.

Despite the contradictions between work and home—or, should I say, the similarities—my life was back on track. I considered myself very intelligent, but I ultimately chose to use my physical strength to make a good living. Better yet, I was my own man. Dad couldn't fault me for being a loser anymore. In fact, it was quite the contrary. Thanks to Anthony and his influence, I was somebody again, somebody to be reckoned with, a violent somebody to be feared and respected.

Then it happened, right when I wasn't looking. As usual, it came out of nowhere. I was smashed with a Louisville Slugger, and I was about to see stars! Of course, it was a woman, a woman with beautiful, thick auburn hair, gorgeous, cat-like green eyes, a great smile with pearly white teeth, and a stunning figure. She was a classic Italian woman, tall and slender with olive skin that was soft and silky smooth; she looked like Sophia Loren.

I knew instantly that I had to meet her. I made Anthony aware of my interest in Carla during one of our conversations. Anthony already knew Carla and took it upon himself to play Cupid, introducing her to his new friend, me. Instantly we connected. The chemistry was obvious. We talked, we laughed, and it was clear from that moment forward that she was the woman of my dreams. At least, I thought so at the time.

Carla was beautiful, innocent, and intelligent and attended a local college as an art major. We hit it off extremely well, just as Anthony and I had. Carla and I became a very noticeable couple around town and were nearly inseparable. Early on in our relationship, it didn't matter to her who I was or what I did. She just seemed to care about me, and I was proud to be seen with her, not only because she was gorgeous but also because I truly liked her. She would come into the club with her sister and friends, turn many men's heads, and stay for hours just to dance, chat with her girlfriends, and be close to me.

There was no way to shield Carla from the blatant violence that was my bread and butter. With her at the club so often, she was bound to see me in action. One night she watched me beat several guys and physically throw one man out the back door and into a dumpster.

The dance floor was full on the night of the infamous dumpster episode, which meant many of the tables around the club were empty. I noticed one particular man going from table to table. It was odd that the man would sit for a short while and glance around the club as if he were people watching. Then I saw him nonchalantly slip his hand into a woman's purse. It was the wrong thing to do in this club, and it was the last thing Anthony wanted happening to any of his customers.

At this point, I leaned over to Carla and said, "Look at the guy at that table over there!" As the club's head bouncer, I was going to take care of business, exactly what was expected from me. Very calmly, I walked over to the table, slammed my hand over the man's hand in the purse, and said in a loud, commanding voice, "What the hell are you doing? I know this isn't your purse!" He gave me a look that said he knew this wasn't going to be his favorite night out on the town.

Grabbing him by the collar, I dragged him to the back door. "You don't do crap like that in this place!" I said. I slapped him in the head a couple of times and then kicked open the back door and threw him over the rail into the dumpster at the base of the stairs. I leaned over the railing to see if he was moving. Then I walked back inside the club, closed the door, and returned to my girlfriend like nothing had happened.

Little did I know that the purse thief I'd just thrown into a dumpster was the nephew of a notorious mob boss in town—not just any boss but a major player. Anthony and I didn't find this out until a few days later, when a few gruff, big-bellied guys, known to everyone in the city, stopped by the club to find out what happened.

It was like a scene from a mob movie. Anthony had a "sit down" with these guys and explained what his bouncer did to the purse thief. I wasn't privy to the conversation, but I could overhear most of what was being said. The men occasionally pointed at me and nodded. I was the guy who'd disrespected one of their own, and it was understood that I could be in some serious trouble if they decided to make any.

I overheard one of them say, "Hey, it's nothing personal. I'm just doing my job." When you hear those words, you really start to think about the kind of life you're leading. I knew it was going to end pretty darn quick or become very uncomfortable for a long time. It sent little cold fish running through my veins and gave me the empty feeling in my gut that I had as a kid when I heard, "Wait till your father gets home and hears about this!"

As the two messengers shook hands with Anthony and walked out the door, I gulped nervously, thinking that my life was going out that door with them. I was a small-time strong arm and knew what Anthony would have had me do in a similar situation.

What was to prevent the upper-level management, so to speak, from inflicting the same type of swift and unforgiving punishment on me? I knew I might get a surprise on a night when I least expected it.

As the week went by, the incident still fresh in my mind, Anthony and I were surprised not to have any unannounced visitors or even hear anything from the two guys. We both thought it had all blown over. But a week later, just when I thought I might be home free, the two guys came walking through the door. This time they'd brought some company: their boss.

This was it. There was no doubt in my mind. I was almost certain I was going for a one-way ride to the hospital. I didn't think I was going to disappear or anything like that, but I was convinced I was in for a beating, something along the lines of, "Listen, pal, we don't want to break your legs, but, if we let you slide, how will it look? Everyone will want to dump the boss's nephew into dumpsters, and we can't have that, now can we? So, kid, which should we break first? The right or the left?"

Anthony greeted the small group and paid his respects while I waited at the bar. A short conversation ensued, and all three men casually left the club, just like that. Anthony walked over to me and smiled. At last I felt a sense of relief.

Anthony had a cat-that-caught-the-rat look on his face as he said, "The big guy said we did the right thing. If he ever hears of his nephew stealing a few dollars out of purses like a cheap punk again, he'd break his hands personally!"

What a relief! I faced the bar and said to Anthony, "Thanks for backing me up. I thought I was in for a beating!" I'd gotten my reprieve, what was better known as "a pass." A thinking man might have taken the near-death experience as a wake-up call to change his ways forever. But I really only thought about one thing: which combo I'd use first, two lefts and a right or two rights and a left.

Little changed in my life over the next year, and life seemed like a novel or a TV show. I had my beautiful girlfriend, Carla, and was making serious money. And Anthony had himself one hell of a bouncer, friend, or bodyguard—I wasn't sure what to call myself—and we all were living one hell of a life. One hell of a life, that is, until one cool, early summer evening in June of 1975. That night, our one hell of a life went all to hell, and I found out that the only good thing about rock bottom is that there's nowhere to go but up.

Anthony pulled me aside to the back bar one night. As we sat together on the stools as we had many times before, Anthony leaned over while carefully looking out over the bar and told me in a low voice that I needed to fix a problem. Evidently Anthony had a problem with a couple of guys named Tommy and Paulie, who were starting to muscle in on Anthony's business or were causing some friction. Exactly what the problem was didn't matter to me; I was loyal to Anthony, and if Anthony needed a favor, I was going to solve the problem before the night was over. It was that simple—or so I thought.

Tommy and Paulie were young Italians, probably considered handsome by some women because of their privileged circumstances in the construction business. Tommy owned a huge home in a very affluent community, his nearest neighbor a couple hundred feet away; his house was set back off a rural road, surrounded by tall pine and maple trees. Anthony and I stood out as well. We drove flashy sports cars and weren't embarrassed to flaunt our social status around town. Despite our material comforts and flashy lifestyle, we were both fairly normal-looking guys for the 1970s. We had big hair, polyester suits, and silk shirts that we unbuttoned down to our navels, exposing our chest hair; we wore several large gold religious medallions around our necks. We were doing well and had many "friends," and our life was seemingly going well until we suddenly acquired a new problem. Unfortunately for Tommy and Paulie, the problem was them.

Anthony's loyal crew of three not-so-small men hastily planned our mission as we drove to Tommy's house. There was the typical bickering in the car about how we should execute this favor. This wasn't the best-planned operation by any means; but what would you expect from three guys who worked in a bar and had limited knowledge of operational planning? Tommy was the main target and was supposed to get the full force of the so-called "worldly lesson." For some reason, he and Anthony were having some type of serious problem, but it wasn't up to any of the three of us doing the beatings to ask why. We just had to do the favor.

We parked the getaway car down the street from Tommy's driveway but close enough to make a fast escape if one were needed. We three "commandos" decided to sneak up between Tommy's house and the next-door neighbor's house under the cover of darkness and then maneuver around to the front and simply walk through the front door. The planning wasn't rocket science, but it was a plan nonetheless, and we were going to execute it. Why not just walk straight up the front walkway and through the front door? Why make the obvious so unobvious? We had no camouflage paint or camouflage fatigues; rather, we were all dressed in polyester walking suits and platform shoes. We also carried baseball bats.

As we stealthily approached the front door, we could hear the music of Donna Summer singing "Turn the Beat Around." This was our chance to enter through the unlocked front door. Our cautious entrance was perfect. There sat Paulie, Tommy's friend, who, unfortunately for him, was in the wrong place at the wrong time. He sat listening to the music on the sofa, his back to us. The music was blaring from the speakers, but Paulie, for some reason, was wearing stereo headphones that were squashing his huge, dirty blond Afro. From the side it appeared as if he were wearing a small saddle on his head. The music drowned out our entrance, and Paulie heard only the voice of Donna Summer.

We flanked the sofa, two of us on one side and one on the other. Paulie immediately noticed us out of the corner of his eye. He stood up in surprise, ripped the headphones off his head, and turned to his left, where he saw two of us with baseball bats. Looking for an escape route, he peered over his right shoulder and saw the third man. At this point, Paulie must have been thinking that it wasn't looking good for the home team. His eyes widened, and he pleaded in a trembling voice, "I won't say anything!" That's when one of us laid into Paulie with the baseball bat, saying, "Damn right you won't say anything!" I didn't know if Paulie heard it, but he definitely felt it. Because it happened so fast, Paulie never had a chance to raise his hands and protect himself. The crack of the bat on Paulie's head sent him spinning to the floor like one of Mike Tyson's second-round knockouts.

As he lay motionless on the floor, blood started to ooze from the side of his head. That image burned itself into my brain. A cold chill ran through my body. Had we just killed Paulie?

There was one man down, possibly dead, but my fellow wise guys and I needed to resume our mission. We needed to find Tommy and deliver a serious message before he made a quick exit or called for backup. We quietly searched the huge house room by room and then quietly walked downstairs to the basement, where we could hear water running in a bathroom. We slowly opened the door, and there was Tommy, standing at the bathroom sink, looking in the mirror as he shaved. Two of us carefully peered around the door. Tommy glanced in the mirror, looked over his shoulder, and spotted us—and there was that look in his eyes, the look that expressed the fear of death. The door slammed open, and without any hesitation, one of my partners and I rushed into the bathroom and delivered an immediate *crack!* The sound of the bat splitting Tommy's head open was now a very recognizable sound. Thud after thud rang out as we hit Tommy over his back, shoulders, and his head, while he attempted to protect himself as best he could.

Tommy received blow after blow from the bat as he scrambled on the floor, attempting to escape the powerful hands of his adversaries. His attempts to get out of the bathroom were unsuccessful, and his fingernails screeched across the tile floor as we dragged him back into the bathroom by his feet and ankles. We yanked him up by his hair as he screamed for help and then threw him into the glass shower door, which shattered into thousands of sharp pieces. There was a loud crash from the glass as it hit the bathroom and shower floors. Our feet crackled on the glass as we continued to administer the beating.

It was a scene I'd been through several times before. Nevertheless, this one was different; I was being paid to administer the violence not as a bouncer but as a strong arm. There was no emotional involvement or attachment to Tommy or Paulie, and, more importantly, it wasn't me on the receiving end.

We weren't supposed to kill or even maim Tommy; we were just supposed to deliver enough of a beating to make him understand that he was vulnerable to another visit by Anthony anytime, anywhere. When we thought he'd had enough, we were to make a quick escape back through the front door, down the driveway, and out to the street. Unfortunately, luck wasn't on our side that night as we darted to the getaway car. As we were making our great escape, I saw headlights rapidly closing in behind us.

The blinding high beams from the car that trailed closely behind us were annoying; most drivers would have chosen to display a universal hand gesture at this point. Having a vehicle closely shadow us was a big surprise. In a few minutes, a glaring, bright blue set of revolving lights on a local police car signaled us to pull over. We pulled our car off to the shoulder and nervously waited for a police officer to approach the driver's window.

The headlights from the police cruiser were shining brightly, lighting up the entire back of the car like the powerful spotlights of the one-time inescapable perimeter of Alcatraz. The lights blinded me as I looked through the back window to see what was going on. A loud, commanding voice shouted, "Step out of the vehicle and put your hands on the roof." I could see only the barrel of what appeared to be a handgun wedged between the door and the body of the police cruiser. A single officer was waiting for backup while crouching behind his car door. My associates and I followed the officer's directions and stepped out of the vehicle. Several other cruisers came to a screeching halt, surrounding my friends and me. Immediately, the officers approached the getaway car with their weapons drawn and began to search us. They slapped on the handcuffs, read us our rights, and moved us into the backseat of a police cruiser. It was a life-changing moment for me, but obviously a day late and a dollar short. I recognized the seriousness of my involvement and the impact it was going to have on my future.

I knew I needed to get out of the business. If I didn't, I was destined for prison or, worse, an early grave. The sheen of the past year's affluent lifestyle now seemed unimportant.

Take away the fancy suits, the fat bank account, the flashy cars, and the gorgeous dame, and who did you have? The same guy who'd showed up at Anthony's bar begging for a job and getting free drinks in return. I was the epitome of a big-time loser and fit the classic definition perfectly: no education, a broken football player, a small-time thug about to spend several years in prison for breaking and entering and assault with a dangerous weapon.

To say that I wasn't very proud of myself was an understatement. Scratch that: it was the understatement of the year.

To my surprise, a few days later, after my arrest and a night in jail, my dad showed up at the nightclub with two of his good friends. My father wasn't making a social call; he didn't want to meet my friends or see anything about my life. The visit was regarding my arrest. Evidently, he'd read the story on the front page of the largest newspaper in the state and wanted to know what was going on and why I hadn't been home lately.

A propensity for violence wasn't the only thing I'd inherited from the old man. I had a very cocky attitude with him in front of his friends. I was on my own territory now, and I'd be damned if I was going to let my father embarrass me in front of my friends. My father actually asked me if there was anything he could do, which surprised me. However, I was only seeing the man—the damage he'd done, the baggage he'd brought with him—not hearing his words. I said, "Don't worry about anything; it's all under control. Everything is taken care of. This will get fixed, trust me."

Dad asked me if I needed any money. Looking at him with a smirk, I said, "Thanks, Dad, but I think I'm okay with money. Matter of fact, why don't you let me buy you guys a round of drinks?" I did everything I could to push my father away from me that night. He surely felt the distance.

Deep inside, Dad was completely embarrassed that his son was in the newspaper for an alleged crime. This time the "Man Mountain of Steel" was obviously not making a public appearance as a football celebrity but as someone who was arrested and accused of breaking the law. My father had never thought he'd see such a thing from his football-hero son. When I stopped to think about it, this was surely breaking my mother's heart as well. Since when did my dad feel that way about hurting my mother? It was about time I took a serious look at myself in the mirror.

Fortunately for me, Tommy decided he'd leave the state to find a better—and safer—place to live. He was never seen or heard from again.

Paulie showed up for the trial and came down with a convenient case of amnesia; suddenly he didn't recognize us. The judge looked at Paulie, politely asked him to stand, and said, "Do you recognize any of these men?"

Paulie quickly replied, "No, sir, I do not. Sir, I don't know these guys, I don't want to know these guys, and I have never seen these guys. I just want to go home and be with my family."

I knew we were home free. A smile of relief lit up my face, partially because the charges were dropped and I was free. More importantly, I realized that I'd just been given another chance; surely that was obvious only to me. The judge then had a conference at the bench with our attorney and the prosecutor and asked them to return to their seats. The judge then called my name and asked me to stand up. He looked directly at me and said, "Son, what do you do?"

I replied politely, "Sir, I am a student at the university."

The judge removed his glasses and, using them to point at me, responded, "Then go back to school, son, finish your education, stay out of trouble, and don't ever let me see you in my court again! Do I make myself clear?"

I immediately responded with a sigh of relief, "Yes, sir!"

The judge put his glasses back on and said, "You are free to go."

He also let my two associates free that day, with no criminal record. I was extremely fortunate. Although I didn't realize it at the time, someone was watching over me. It wasn't my dad but it might have been my father. I didn't recognize it right away, but I would come to believe it soon, very, very soon.

The violence, the arrest, the visit from Dad, the abbreviated trial—they all seemed to be harbingers of change. Over the next year, Carla and I became closer than ever; she had given me her undivided support. We'd seriously talked on many occasions about a future together, but I felt I needed to change my life for the better. I just wasn't sure how I was going to do it.

Anthony and I started to slowly part ways as I began to think about a better way of life. A separation was inevitable, and though it was wishful thinking, I hoped it would be amiable. I no longer wanted to be someone's "boy." I no longer saw the glamour in being a tough guy. Being a tough guy wasn't going to keep me out of jail or keep me from getting seriously hurt, beaten up, or killed. Anthony didn't like the fact that he was losing his right-hand man. He became more demanding, while I became more resistant. A power struggle was occurring, and I knew I had to bail out while our tempers were still at a favorable temperature.

Living part-time with Anthony needed to end, and staying in hotels was no longer affordable, so I once again moved in full-time with my parents; my dad was getting annoyed again regarding my poor job-hunting skills. Every day, my father came home and asked me if I'd found a "real job" yet. The too-familiar smell of alcohol and the belligerent, condescending voice that made me want to throw up signaled his homecoming. I didn't know how much longer I could endure my father's conduct and often wondered how my mother had tolerated this behavior for so many years.

My sister Carol had moved out and attempted to make a life of her own. She'd moved far enough away so that only a brief visit from my dad was possible. Meanwhile, Michael was dealing with marital problems and had a new baby on the way. He and his wife only visited my mother when contact with my dad was going to be minimal, and they usually stayed away on Friday and Saturday.

Despite how poorly Dad treated his family, I was still confused by my love/hate relationship with my father. How could a person treat his family so horribly and yet still have his victims wishing for love from that person? I often wondered if I saw my father in myself. I also wondered if my father understood the legacy he had left for his son, a violent man in a violent world. So many times I wanted to deny my father, to run away and start life over, even change my name; but always I found myself back under his roof. I was my dad, and my dad was me, and we were linked through the twin abuses of violence and failure.

I hated my father, yet it seemed I was destined to become him.

I loved my father, yet I yearned for the day when I could leave him. Sometimes things happen for an unknown reason. One of my best friends from high school decided to return to Rhode Island from California. The timing could not have been more perfect; he arrived just in time to help me make a clean break from my current death trap. Dave was every high school girl's dream, with a quick wit to match. Dave was an attractive, blue-eyed, blond-haired guy with rosy cheeks. He was extremely athletic, with a black belt in Tae Kwon Do. He was an all-American guy with a carefree spirit who had moved to California several years ago in search of wealth and adventure.

I heard he'd returned to Rhode Island and decided to call him to get together for a few beers. Dave and I met at a local bar, reminisced, and talked about our bleak futures. It was somewhat refreshing to know I wasn't the only college dropout the high school had produced. We'd both searched for something better but never found it. Looking at my friend was like looking in a mirror, much too closely and for far too long.

We were both twenty-one years old, hanging out in bars and sleeping most of the day. I was still working for Anthony but making every attempt now to work less, which caused even more friction and deeper resentment. I was still seeing Carla, but that relationship soon started to suffer because of a lack of funds.

Essentially, Dave and I were becoming useless and pathetic. One day, while we were watching television and drinking beer, a commercial for the U.S. Army came on. We looked at each other and said, "Hey, here's a way to get some great benefits and maybe a trade or complete our education. It wouldn't be a bad way for us to get out of here too." I knew my days at home were limited, and I had to do something with my life soon or go back to a life of uncertainty. Dave and I visited the local army recruiter.

Though I wasn't sure I was making a good decision, it turned out to be the best choice I'd ever made. I hoped that by leaving the pseudo-glamorous lifestyle (but not necessarily my beautiful Italian girlfriend) I'd close the door on that way of life forever. If I could leave the club and Anthony without disrespecting him, then joining the army would be a viable and safe option. Eventually I would slip away.

Inevitably, the guys at the club decided to throw me a "going into the army" party, and I really feared it was a "going away forever" party. The bash was at a restaurant and bar outside the city. Everyone from the nightclub was expected to be there, along with some of the top players from Anthony's "family." Was I really so highly rated that someone very powerful would attend a party in my name? It didn't seem right. Something seemed very strange. I'd thought I was never really considered anyone of value with this crew. Now they were celebrating in my honor.

I hadn't seen my brother in a while and asked him if he'd like to go to the party and drive me home. We drove to the restaurant, and I made it perfectly clear that this party may be a "going away forever" party. I looked Michael in the eye and said seriously, "Mike, this may be a going-away party, but it may be the kind where the guest of honor doesn't make it home—ever. You know that Anthony and I have had some serious problems over the past few months, and he has a significant amount of power. So if they decide to take me for a ride somewhere, just get in my car, drive away, and never look back or ask any questions. You understand me? Say you understand me!"

Mike immediately said, "What the hell are you talking about?" He clearly didn't know where this conversation was going and was clueless about what I was telling him. He knew I was in over my head with something, but what was

I asking? Maybe Mike wanted to keep his head in the sand. We'd both grown up wishing away the ill in this world, closing our eyes during our father's many violent bouts of rage and hoping it would all just go away.

I pulled the car into the parking lot of the restaurant and said in a calm voice, "Do you understand me? If anything happens to me, just let it happen and forget about it. Do you understand? You don't need to get involved in any of this, okay? Just let it happen the way it's supposed to happen. I just don't want anything to happen to you. You're not involved in any of this. You just need to have a good time, meet some people I work with, and enjoy the party. If I get too drunk, then you need to take me home."

Mike nodded, but I wasn't reassured.

As we entered into the restaurant's party hall, cheers and applause came from everyone, including Anthony. There was an elaborate spread of Italian food and drinks. I received handshake after handshake, pats on the back, and affectionate pinches on my cheeks. It was clear that everyone genuinely wished me well.

I partied through the night. Evidently, I'd made my problems with Anthony more of a big deal than they really were. The party went on all night and into the early morning. They were feeding me shots laced with who knew what, and I could barely see or stand. Sometime during the night, I told my brother to go home and that I'd see him the next day. Michael left the party and headed home, thinking everything was going to be alright. They'd baptized me, but in the back of my mind, I was thinking about the possible outcome of the evening.

Although I was accepting this celebration with reckless abandon, I mentally prepared myself to accept whatever fate I'd face that evening. The large amount of alcohol I'd consumed made it much easier for me to concede the destiny that possibly awaited me. I still cannot remember most of what happened during that drunken, blurry night.

Surely, I would have remembered something, especially the guys who drove me home or that I heard my Doberman Pincher, Gypsy, barking and growling at the front door. When we arrived at my parents' home, it was early the next morning. One of them rang the doorbell, while the other guys carried the soon-to-be army basic trainee by the arms and leaned me over the wooden rail fence that surrounded our small home.

My mother came to the door with the dog and recognized a few of my friends.

"Hello, guys! I guess he's not doing too well, huh?" They replied briefly; they had no intention of tangling with Gypsy, and they quickly got in their car. She could hear some of them say things like, "He had a great time, and we're gonna miss da big guy!"

As my mom came out to help me inside, the guys sped off, saying "Sorry, Mrs. Gouin. He'll be okay in da morning!"

My father didn't come out to help because he was in his own Friday stupor as usual.

I rose later the next day. My head felt like it was a basketball bouncing on the court. I realized that the party had been just a party—truly for me, John Gouin. It had been a genuine going-away party, not the kind of party I'd feared. As it turned out, all my apprehension was for naught. Chalk it up to too many mob movies and not enough confidence in the general charity of modern man.

Later that week, after my liver and brain had completely recovered from the alcohol saturation, Dave and I were in the recruiter's office, raising our right hands and swearing to uphold the Constitution of the United States of America. It was a long, winding, and treacherous road that ultimately directed me to the army, and soon I was reporting to Fort Dix, New Jersey. It had been a tough road that was full of potholes, pit stops, speed bumps, and danger zones.

Now I was finally ready to get off this broken highway and travel the straight and narrow road to a more normal existence.

Chapter 6: *Wooden Soldier*

People sleep peaceably in their beds at night only because rough men stand ready to do violence on their behalf.

~ **George Orwell**

It was the evening after I'd raised my right hand at the local army recruiting station. Our matchbox-size house was filled with the routine nervous apprehension that anticipated Dad's arrival. Goodwill was short-lived in our house, and you could feel the tension slowly mounting, despite the beautiful summer evening sky. Like clockwork, Dad strolled through the front door at his usual time and in his usual condition. There was no "Hello everybody, I'm home!" Instead, he said, "I'm hungry. What's to eat?" I rolled my eyes; my body tensed up, and my teeth clenched in expectation of what could possibly happen that night. I looked at my mother. Her wonderful smile faded, and her face paled.

His threatening, domineering voice no longer affected me the way it had when I was a child. I was more than ready to respond to any form of my father's belligerent, condescending verbal mistreatment. My physical stature and maturity now prevented the physical abuse, but after years and years of psychological intimidation, fear still lurked in the back of my mind. I'm sure he was eager to launch a barrage of insulting comments and nerve-wracking questions, hoping I'd take the bait again. I was absolutely positive and thankful to God that it wasn't going to be a question about a football official. Of course, this time I was fully prepared to answer his question regarding the difference between the referee and the umpire.

He sat down and stared across the table at me with a look that telegraphed trouble. With his head hanging down, he said in a loud, sarcastic voice, "Since you're working less and less for Anthony, did you get a job yet? You need to start bringing some money into this house if you're going to live here! You're not going to be a freeloader. There are no free rides here, buddy!"

As he continued to bellow at me, his voice slowly faded. In my mind, I wandered off, back to the summer when I was sixteen. I'd started my very first job, working in a textile factory. I made $1.65 per hour, $0.15 cents *over* minimum wage. Dad's selective memory had obviously erased how hard I'd worked in that sweatbox during the summer months in high school. He may have forgotten, but my mother and I surely had not. The factory was a non-air-conditioned building full of hazardous materials. And OSHA? OSHA wasn't even a consideration back then.

Powdered chemical dyes filled the air as I prepared to color the raw worsted textile materials. When the dye made contact with moisture, such as the sweat on your skin, it would spread, leaving streaks on your face and arms. The different colors made you look like something out of a haunted house. It usually took several days to wash off the streaks and starburst speckles of malachite green, safranin red, and gentian violet. Until then, it was like walking around with a colorful reflective coating that itched and flaked day and night.

My close high school friends who didn't have to work usually came by once or twice a week at lunchtime, taunting, tempting, and coaxing me into going to the beach. I learned a sense of responsibility at an early age. If I missed work and lost income for the family, I could expect physical consequences from my father. It was absolute torture for a sixteen-year-old, knowing my friends were enjoying the cool ocean water and warm breeze of the Atlantic while I was working in a sweatbox for almost nothing. There was absolutely no way I could escape and call in sick. Dad followed the time on my weekly paycheck stub very closely. At sixteen, my life revolved around two angry, controlling pit bosses: one at work and one at home.

Sometimes I didn't know which was worse.

I could complain all I wanted, but come Monday morning I was right back at the plant bright and early. I always tried to get just a few minutes of overtime. There were no other choices for this hard-working young man. It was a job, and, more importantly, it was the only way to pitch in and help support our family. Of course, my father only saw my weekly contribution as extra income, not as my blood, sweat, and sacrifice. That figures. When you make the rules, you can stack the deck in your favor.

Of course, Dad kept all his extra money from refereeing football games and gambling. Nobody ever knew how large an account he had from his additional income-generating activities, and we dared not ask. It seemed logical that if I worked overtime I should be able to keep any additional money beyond my regular paycheck and allowance. That would be comparable to Dad keeping his extra income. Each week I gave my entire paycheck to my mother, and, in return, I received the same small allowance back. So why should I work extra hours if there was no benefit to me?

In the real world, it's a simple equation: you work hard, and it pays off. That wasn't true in our house. There was a definite double standard, and, like most of Dad's "laws," it was not to be challenged. I wished I'd given more to my mother and complained about it less often. I understand today that our family was poor, but I didn't know then that we were. I never understood the concept until I entered high school and met a girl whose parents were affluent, according to my standards. My girlfriend's parents had their own home with central air-conditioning, which is rare in New England, an above-ground swimming pool, and a two-car garage. Until I went to high school, my world consisted only of our low-income neighborhood and my local friends. Anything outside that world was virtually nonexistent.

It is something that you never quite comprehend as a child until you reach adulthood. I was angry with my father. I resented giving most of my hard-earned sweatshop money to my father but never fully understood how much of that money actually went to my mother to help her support the family. How much easier did my contributions make her day-to-day struggle? If only I'd known how much of a difference my financial contributions made to our meager lifestyle. As children become adults, we begin to see the light; and when we become parents, we understand adult responsibilities much too late. Had I known what I know now, I probably would have sailed through a long, hard, laborious summer without a single complaint and worked additional hours to contribute more to our family.

And so it goes. As most parents have said at one time or another, "Wait until you have your own family; then you'll understand." Usually we don't comprehend our childhood actions until we actually reach adulthood, or until we have our own children and reality sets in. Realistically, that money was used for many necessities, such as new clothes for school, food, and even rent. All of this made my mother's life easier; my job made Mom's life easier. When school started back up, I realized that if I was going to go to college, I needed to get a scholarship desperately. Football became my answer. Unfortunately, that didn't turn out as I'd hoped and dreamed.

As I slowly began to tune back in to my father's voice, I looked at Dad and said confidently, "Don't worry. I got a job!"

His jaw dropped and he remarked sarcastically, "What? *You? Found a job?* Well, it's about damn time! What the hell are *you* going to do? Work in a factory again?"

I leaned back in the chair and said, "I'm going to carry an M16."

Dad responded with a snickering laugh. "You're going to do what? Carry an M16?"

I knew that response would raise an eyebrow. If anyone knew what an M16 was, it was my old man. "Yes, Dad," I said. "I joined the army, and I'm going to be an airborne infantry soldier! I'm leaving with Dave next month for Fort Dix, New Jersey. You remember that base, don't you, Dad? That's where you and Michael were both stationed for basic training. The two of you were in the army, and I suppose it's just something I have to do." Dad was in the army just after World War II and during Korea. Mike was drafted during Vietnam and was stationed at Fort Rucker, Alabama.

Dad looked at me for a beat, unblinking. Then he rolled out one of his famous backhanded compliments and let it fill the air with the pungent scent of implied failure. "It'll be good for you. It'll teach you some discipline, but you probably aren't going to last a week. You'll probably get into a fight or kick the shit out of your drill sergeant and end up in the brig. I know your temper! You'll be right back home before you know it."

I knew exactly where my father was going with this. He was referring to my failed football career. Since I didn't make it to the NFL and never finished college, why should I make it through basic training? Was my father trying to push me into doing something with my life, or was he just dissatisfied and disgusted with a son who was turning into the epitome of a big-time loser?

Worse yet, where did I really stand throughout this whole ordeal? For whom and why was I actually doing this?

Myself?

Or, on the other hand, was it for my father?

I thought about how rash I'd been to enlist as a private. What was I thinking? I watched an army commercial on television while drinking beer at two o'clock in the afternoon with an old friend, and, just like that, we went down to the recruiting station to sign up. It was like something out of that Bill Murray movie *Stripes*. Nevertheless, the longer I thought about it, the more sense it made. It was a gut feeling, and it just felt right. I'd burned so many bridges, there was nowhere left for me to go. I needed to change my life, change it drastically and change it immediately, before I made any other bad decisions that may prove to be very costly and irreparable.

I gave my father a serious look, a look he'd never seen before, and I said, "You know, Dad, you and Michael were both in the army. Well, I guess it's my turn, and I'm going in with Dave."

We reunited in our hometown after my close encounter with some "goodfellas" and my gradual separation from Anthony. Dave had mastered Tae Kwon Do and went to California hoping to make it to the big time as a rough and tumble actor in the movies or as a karate champion. His fame and success were short-lived, and it never panned out for him, but he was a great guy. Dave was more interested in athletic activities than physical labor. He returned home without any direction. Since we were both lost souls and misery loves company, we got along quite well, always thinking of ways to make money and become financially successful.

Dad said with a sarcastic laugh, "Dave? Son, you really have lost it!" He expressed his usual certainty in my failure.

That was it; end of discussion. Dad simply stood up and walked away from the kitchen table to watch television in another room. Yet I was still so excited about the adventure I was about to embark on. And Dad? Well, the conversation didn't seem to faze him at all.

On the other hand, maybe it had. I was still sitting at the table, reviewing the information I'd received from the recruiter, when my father entered the kitchen. Dad sat back down at the table without saying a word. Thirty minutes later, he started the conversation again and said, "John, if you want, I can get you out of this commitment. I know some people who can help us!"

Without hesitation, I immediately replied, "Thanks, Dad. I appreciate your interest, but this is something I have to do. Don't worry; I'll be okay." I was shocked that my father had asked me that question. There was no turning back, and my head and eyes were facing forward. I was at the point of no return. If Dad knew anything about me, it was that I was determined. He was fully aware that I was not a quitter. So what was my father really trying to accomplish?

My father's comments always left a trail of questions in their wake. Was he trying to humiliate me by insinuating that I couldn't handle the army? Did he think I didn't have the character to deal with those long days and weeks of being miserable, lonely, hungry, and tired? On the other hand, was he sincere and genuinely concerned for his son's well-being? Either way, I was going to push forward with my new adventure. I was going to prove to my father that I could succeed at something, anything, but also prove it to myself as well.

Making good on my promise to survive basic training was one thing; but some other issues required attention. There were the obvious long-standing problems with my father, but I had to face some more serious phobias as well. I'd been hiding them all my life. My physical stature as a child may have been intimidating to some kids, but it was no match for a few things that may have appeared simple to them. I was dreadfully afraid of heights, standing or swimming in water deeper than my knees, and being alone in dark places. I wasn't exactly what I would call airborne infantry material and definitely lacked some of the intestinal fortitude I'd need to meet the selection criteria for the Green Beret qualification course.

It was obvious to those around me that I was unsuccessful in hiding my own fears, especially when I stood on a stepladder to change a light bulb. My knees weakened, my hands trembled, and my fear of heights was so overwhelming that facing my father's wrath was a walk in the park in comparison. During an occasional family trip to the beach, wading in waist-deep water was as far as I'd go because I feared the unknown beneath me. Going hiking or camping and sleeping outside in a tent, in the dark, in the woods, alone or even with other people, was impossible. Forget it! There was no way, not me, not Mr. Badass!

Despite my outwardly tough appearance, my fears were a serious weakness for me as an elite soldier. Overcoming these concerns was something I needed to face up to, and the army was going to help. The military was my opportunity to overcome them, free of charge, and I was ready to accept the challenge. Like most obstacles in my life, I was about to take this head-on with a positive attitude and a confident, quiet attitude.

That's exactly how it happened, fast, without hesitation and with no looking back. Three weeks later, there I was on a crowded bus full of basic trainees heading for Fort Dix, New Jersey. I prepared to accept what lay ahead. I was expecting the worst as we arrived at the base and began to offload. My right foot had barely touched the ground when there, poking into my face, was a wide-brimmed Smoky the Bear hat. Under the hat was a man who was yelling so loudly that his face turned red. With every word came a shower of his saliva.

The drill sergeants screamed mercilessly, already doing their jobs and breaking our civilian mentality. However, I was mature enough to know better; getting screamed and yelled at was nothing new to me. It was a flashback of days past with my father, so I wasn't intimidated. I tolerated each insult with little problem. Yes, it was culture shock, but I'd been through this drill many times before; these guys were no different from the coaches who'd screamed at me every football season. In fact, their vitriol was less fearsome than the unrelenting pounding delivered by my father every day of my life.

No matter what they said or how loud they said it, I stayed focused on the thought that no matter what happened to me, it would all be over in eight weeks. I knew in my heart I could tolerate anything for eight weeks, especially anything dished out from a drill sergeant. I understood right from the start that the drill sergeants were not going to kill me—intentionally, at least—and that I should expect to be cold, tired, hungry, wet, and miserable. Attempting to intimidate me only reinforced my determination to succeed and allowed me to focus on what I needed to do: make it through basic training. Above all else, I needed to prove to my father and myself that I was going to be successful at least at something, even if it was just basic training.

Later that first evening, as all the lights in the barracks gradually clicked off one by one, an eerie silence filled the sleeping bay. You could hear the sniffles of some of the younger recruits among the snoring and the usual gastric sounds. As I curled up in my bunk, ready to sleep, I noticed I was having some difficulty with my breathing. Something was wrong, and it was getting worse; I knew what was coming because I'd experienced this problem many times before, especially after the beatings by my father. Gradually, my chest began to tighten as though a boa constrictor were curling around its victim, slowly squeezing the air out of my lungs; my breathing became more and more labor-intensive. It was one of the worst attacks I'd had since I was a child. Of all the times for this to happen, why did it have to be on the very first night in basic training? There was no way I was going to be sent home. There was just no way. I was not going back to be ridiculed by my father and hear him say how right he was about me not lasting more than a week in the army. I closed my eyes. Between gasps, I prayed for divine intervention to help me survive this dreadful night. I convinced myself that I was okay and that if I really wanted to be in the army then I'd have to work through this problem on my own. I was confident that everything would be alright in the morning, as long as I didn't stop breathing in my sleep.

I just had to put up with the wheezing long enough for it to resolve itself, and everything would be alright. The night seemed endless. With each labored breath, I felt myself get weaker and weaker. Fatigue began to close in as my chest tired and my eyes slowly began to close. I kept reiterating to myself, *I can make it through this, I can make it through this, and I am not going home!*

Refusing to seek medical attention and not getting any sleep made for a bad way to start my first day of basic training. As the morning sun began to rise, I found myself feeling extremely fatigued, but I knew everything was alright. I was able to breathe much better, notwithstanding the fact that I was overly concerned about having a relapse within the next few hours. If a relapse did occur, there was no way I'd be able to hide my labored breathing from the drill sergeants. They'd force me to visit the medical clinic for evaluation and treatment, and they'd eventually medically board me out and put me on the next bus home.

Slam! Bang! The sound of trashcans turning over and their lids flying across the sleeping bay echoed loudly. "Get up, first call!" shouted the drill sergeants. Without warning, the crashing trash cans and roaring drill sergeants yelling for everyone to get out of their bunks forced me to quickly roll out of bed and begin my new routine as an army recruit.

Although the result could have been fatal, persisting through the night helped me develop a greater sense of inner strength and determination. I acquired a more positive attitude, which would help me endure the rocky road that lay ahead over the next several months and years. Coming home with my tail between my legs or looking in the mirror and seeing a failure or a quitter wasn't an option for me.

As it turns out, my greatest fears were unfounded. Basic training was not as difficult as I had expected. Day after day, challenge after challenge, I calmly held my head up, kept my mouth shut, and did exactly as I was told.

If a drill sergeant ordered me to crawl in the mud face first, I didn't question him; I placed my body on the cold ground and crawled in the mud face first. The path to leadership began at the bottom. I first had to learn to take orders before I could give them.

I was slowly becoming what the drill sergeants wanted me to become: a soldier, a leader.

I was quickly becoming what I felt I needed to become: a soldier, a man.

Drill sergeants are trained to produce well-disciplined, high-quality soldiers and to recognize candidates with potential leadership skills. They have the faculty to develop an individual with an aptitude to take command and the willingness to assume responsibility. Whatever their reasoning, the drill sergeants identified me as a soldier with promise. Although my clouded past was casting a shadow of doubt over my confidence, I wasn't about to refuse an opportunity. Maybe I was being naïve, but I readily accepted the challenge. They were determined to extract my potential skills and process them into some semblance of a leader at the basic level of soldiering.

People took notice, and they were the right people this time. The drill sergeants eventually singled me out and placed me in positions of accelerating leadership, first as a squad leader then as a platoon guide. It seemed as if I was getting back into my football-playing mode, being recognized for my small but notable accomplishments. It was different from the stellar attention of the local newspapers back home. I was now feeling a sense of accomplishment and pride, although some things never changed: nothing was ever good enough for my dad and me. No matter how well I performed, I had to do better and better. I had that insatiable need again, the desire to excel. I could never be second best. I just couldn't.

Eventually, other soldiers approached me for help on soldier skills and even personal problems. I took the time to help my classmates with any problems or questions they had. I had the foresight to realize that maybe one day I'd be going to war with these soldiers, so I was motivated to help them as much as possible. It was important to me to get to know and understand each and every one of them.

I felt exhilarated by my newly found leadership skills. To be looked up to and admired by my fellow soldiers was a thrill, even more than scoring a touchdown or nailing a lineman on the field. This was true camaraderie in every sense of the word. It was a hard adjustment at first, shouldering responsibility not only for myself but also for the team, where every member depended on one another. However, eventually I got used to it. Maybe it was what I subconsciously desired; possibly, it was what I was destined to achieve. It all seemed so natural.

I thought about it as little as possible. Like always, I just put my head and eyes forward and never looked back. Finishing as an honor graduate out of both basic and infantry training was certainly a surprise to my father and especially to me, but again, it just happened so naturally. As graduation from basic training approached, I phoned home and asked Mom and Dad if they'd come to watch me graduate. I could hear the excitement in their voices as they readily agreed.

A few days later, they sat in the audience and proudly watched me receive several military awards. Suddenly, right in the middle of the ceremony, one drill sergeant walked up to me, now PFC Gouin, and told me to stand up and start singing in front of the entire audience, about five hundred people and soldiers. My parents were very surprised when I began to sing inspiring military songs in front of the entire auditorium. Singing and standing in front of an audience, drawing attention to myself, was not my forte, but I did it and, surprisingly, did it well.

Basic and infantry training were challenging, but moving on to the dreaded and fearful airborne training was another story altogether. I was determined to conquer my fear of heights. As the bus from infantry school pulled up to the airborne training school, I looked up at the 250-foot training tower, knowing that one day in the near future I'd jump from this one-time carnival ride. All my phobias and fears seemed to surround this nearly indescribable feat: a fear of heights, water, and being alone in dark places. They were practically buzzwords from the airborne brochure!

My primary objective was simply to finish the training and overcome my fear of heights. Anything else would just be gravy. I maintained my philosophy that I should take it one day at a time. I wanted to simply make it through this next military school and attack my next fear. I wanted to wear the army parachute badge as a constant reminder of my accomplishment and success. The training was grueling and physically demanding, but with every new day, I accepted a new challenge and eventually overcame each one. At the end of three weeks of training, I'd face the ultimate test: jump out of an airplane five times—without wetting my pants—and land safely without breaking an ankle.

The day finally came when I stepped outside the barracks and began to prepare myself for my first parachute jump. My mind-set was similar to what we called "pre-game jitters" before a football game. I had to psyche myself up! There was nervous, quiet chatter among the soon-to-be paratroopers. I stood alone, taking in the early morning rays of sunlight that began to break through the horizon in the eastern Georgia sky. I noticed the droplets of dew scattered over the freshly cut grass dancing in the cool breeze.

That morning, I acquired a greater sense of appreciation for life's splendor, glory, and natural beauty, as well as the little things it has to offer. There was something very precious about my experience, which helped me understand what I'd been overlooking for many years; all that time, the precious gift of life had been staring me right in the face. It's amazing how you begin to accept and treat it dearly when you think the end may be near. I was about to overcome my greatest fear with the rising of the winter sun.

At the hangar, the pre-jump checklists started, and my heart rate began to increase. Despite the cooler weather outside the huge sliding aluminum doors of the hangar, I began to sweat. Dave and I had completed basic and infantry training together, and now we were about to bring an end to Jump School. We went through our pre-jump inspections, checking the helmet, shoulder harnesses, and leg straps. We checked an important part of our parachute gear, the static line, a thick yellow nylon cord connecting the parachute to the airplane that automatically pulls the parachute out of the bag when the parachutist exits the aircraft. We checked it repeatedly and thoroughly for any tears or signs of dry rot. We, along with the rest of the future jumpers, were finally strapped into our parachutes and sat back to back on the hangar floor. There was nothing but dead silence until I turned my head and whispered to my friend, "Dave, what the hell are we doing? Are we really going to jump out of an airplane at 1,250 feet, right after the sun comes up? Are we out of our minds, or what?" Dave had little to say, and I could barely see him shaking his head in disgust, as if we were both doomed.

The thunderous and forceful command to load the aircraft was given from the "Black Hats," the name given to the airborne instructors who wore black baseball caps with rank and a set of jump wings pinned to the front. As Dave, the rest of the troopers, and I stood up and shuffled to board the cold, camouflage C-123 aircraft, I noticed that the seats were made of red nylon netting and that there was barely enough room to stand, never mind move around. It felt as though we were cattle going to the slaughter. The doors slammed shut, the engines roared, the nose of the aircraft lifted, and we were soon skyward. I peered out the porthole and could see orange streaks of the sun as it peeked over the horizon. I gazed at its magnificent splendor.

The aircraft slowed to stall speed, and the wings tilted up and down as it maneuvered into position over the drop zone. This was it. There was only one way out as far as I was concerned, and there was no turning back. Although I was extremely nervous and definitely afraid, which I probably wouldn't have admitted at the time, I felt completely prepared and ready for the pre-jump commands to begin. As I stared at Dave sitting across from me, I was startled by the shouting of the commands to prepare to jump, but I started the entire process just as I'd trained for over the last three weeks. The training drills had made my actions instinctual, and I was going to follow all the commands just as I'd been trained.

The doors opened, and the cold winter air rushed into the aircraft, stirring the dust and sand on the cabin floor. My eyes were wide open and glued to the warning light on the wall next to the exit door. Organized chaos filled the aircraft as we waited and watched for the light to change from red to green. The visual signal alerts the jumpmaster to begin exiting the jumpers from the aircraft. Adrenaline was pumping through my veins as I made a last-minute mental check of everything I'd been trained to do.

The light flashed green, and the jumpers began shuffling toward the rear of the aircraft. I could barely hear the commands over the engines' noise, the rushing wind, and the shuffling of footsteps on the floor of the fuselage. The commands "Go! Go! Go!" were shouted by the jumpmaster as each trooper exited the aircraft. The engines roared louder and louder with each step I took toward the exit door.

As I moved closer to the rear of the aircraft, a warm blast of air slammed against my face. I approached the door with an airborne shuffle, looked directly at the jumpmaster, handed him my static line, and heard him shout, "Go!" I followed his command, just as I'd been trained to do over the past few weeks. As I took that huge first step out the door of the C-123 airplane, I closed my eyes. In fact, I closed them so tightly I thought I was making a jump at night. I hopped out of the aircraft and could feel myself falling as I counted *one thousand, two thousand, three thousand.* Then I felt the sudden jolt of the parachute inflating above me. It was the signal that everything was going as planned, a successful first step.

Before I opened my eyes, I could hear and feel the stillness and beauty of floating through air. Slowly opening my eyes to a squint, I could see for miles. The cool morning breeze broke the calm and quiet of this unique sense of peacefulness. I was completing my first parachute jump, and the ground appeared to rise rapidly toward me. My fear of heights had been confronted. I screamed with excitement, "I did it! Airborne!"

Nearly as quickly as the celebration started, the Black Hat on the ground ended it. He yelled through his megaphone, "Okay, you're airborne. Now get your ass down here and make your proper parachute landing fall!" The ground seemed to move up to me very rapidly as I prepared to make a proper parachute landing. *Thump!* I hit the ground hard and rolled but not as hard as I'd anticipated. I now had a new sense of pride and accomplishment. Over the next few days, all five of my qualifying jumps went uneventfully for me and for Dave as well. Both of us were now airborne-qualified, wearing parachute wings and on our way to join the infamous Eighty-second Airborne Division as a "Five Jump Chump, a Cherry!"

After approximately eight months of my assignment as a rifleman in an infantry platoon at Fort Bragg, I was starting to get bored. I no longer felt challenged and needed to fill my insatiable appetite for adventure and accomplishment. I'd gotten a taste for excelling in the military, which drove me to volunteer for Special Forces training, one of the most demanding and elite military schools. Both physically and mentally challenging, this training was going to make me one of America's best: a Green Beret.

Back at home, Carla was very content with her life; she still enjoyed the nightlife at the club and continued with her college education. She wrote to me on a regular basis and waited patiently for her tough-guy boyfriend to complete his demanding training. She enjoyed the continued notoriety but missed my constant attention along with the expensive dinners, jewelry, and fine cars. I was convinced she'd found her tall, dark, and handsome man, but I was only her pseudo-hero in the local community, which didn't amount to very much.

That was about to change more for me than for Carla. After about a year of being stationed at Fort Bragg, North Carolina, and in the middle of

Special Forces training, Carla dropped a bombshell right when it could hurt the most.

I received a classic "Dear John" letter from Carla. She was finished waiting for me and had decided to move on with her life. She'd met someone else and made up her mind that she needed immediate affection and attention, which was something I could not provide from North Carolina; I could provide only an occasional phone call and letters containing our dreams of a future together. Money was very tight for me as a private first class, and I needed to be very frugal, considering our future. Prior to joining the army, I shared a generous lifestyle with Carla, fine cars, expensive jewelry, and many other luxuries that were a benefit of my job.

My income went from about $500 a week to about $300 a month; in 1975–1976, that was a significant decrease in pay and a dramatic change in my standard of living. I also had to sell my 1976 Monte Carlo to make ends meet. Carla was spoiled and had difficulty handling the social adjustment. She disliked the feeling of not having her man at her side. She needed to be in the spotlight and ultimately met someone who could afford her the luxury that she thought she deserved.

Going through Special Forces training was difficult enough with its physical and intellectual challenges. But I was also isolated at Camp Mackall a small training post in the western part of Fort Bragg, which was surrounded by tall Carolina pines; there was no civilization for miles. We had no outside contact with anybody, no pizza delivery, no television or any other form of entertainment; it was the perfect environment for producing some of America's best-educated, hardened, and dedicated soldiers, ready to defend this country on a moment's notice.

The only form of communication available was a pay telephone, which was off-limits except when special privileges were granted. The only real means of communication with the outside world was with handwritten letters that sometimes took weeks to be delivered. Now, here I was PFC Gouin, no longer the tough street guy, training in the middle of nowhere, pressured to work harder and harder with less sleep each night, and forced to be cold, tired, hungry, wet, and miserable under extremely stressful conditions. Add in the fact that the woman I was planning on marrying just told me that she'd met another man, and it was good-bye for me.

After receiving that letter, I had difficulty sleeping for the next two months. When I had an opportunity to put my head down, sleep wouldn't come because I continued to think of her. Lying down on a cold steel bunk with no comfortable mattress and no heat in the middle of January just made things worse. I was miserable emotionally and physically, but I had plenty of company in my fellow students.

It was different for me. As I lay there listening to the snoring of tired and worn-out soldiers, I would close my eyes not to sleep but to think about Carla and the great life we were supposed to have, a life that included a home and children. At times, I walked the concrete floors of the small, wooden, windowless, fifteen-man Quonset hut. Like a tiger in a cage, I paced back and forth for several hours in the early morning. I wrapped my poncho liner around my cold shoulders and walked until the sound of "First call!" well before sunrise. This was when every soldier had to get up from his bunk and start a new and exciting day as a Green Beret trainee. "First call" in Special Forces school started with the recorded sound of General Patton's famous speech or the song "The Ballad of the Green Berets."

I had completed nearly half of my training when I finally reached the breaking point. My emotions were overshadowing my sense of responsibility and clouding my judgment. One night, after a long, hard training day, I decided I was going to call it quits. I'd had enough and was going AWOL—not a very wise choice for a soldier hoping to build a military career. I was rapidly spiraling out of control and had the uncontrollable urge to look into Carla's gorgeous green eyes, smell her sensual perfume, and touch her soft skin; I could almost taste her. Knowing there was no way that the pleasure I fantasized and dreamed about with Carla was going to become a reality nearly drove me insane.

I was slowly becoming self-destructive, and I felt so depressed, alone, and abandoned during my isolation and training that I almost forgot it was my twenty-third birthday.

Of course, there were no celebratory birthday wishes from the cadre or my fellow trainees, no cake, no candles, and no gifts. In fact, none of my fellow trainees even knew it was my birthday, and I didn't think that any of them even cared since they were so exhausted from the day's rigorous training.

At around 10 PM, when everyone was supposed to be in their bunks and asleep, I decided I wasn't going to let my birthday slip by without a celebration of some sort. I grabbed my poncho liner, a warm, lightweight, camouflage nylon blanket that was easily transportable, and walked out the front door of the sleeping hut. Since I wasn't sure where to go to avoid being caught, I found a huge pine tree to sit under in a secluded area of the camp where nobody would look for a soldier at that time of night. I sat down and rested my back on the sturdy tree, taking a deep breath and letting out a sigh.

The sky was a deep navy blue, and the stars were twinkling like Carla's eyes had the first time we met. Earlier, I'd rummaged around in my rucksack, the army's equivalent to a civilian's backpack, for my C-rations and found a can of pound cake. I thought this would be a great way for me to celebrate my birthday. When I opened the can, the sweet smell of pound cake overwhelmed the crisp aroma of the southern pines immediately. In every box of C-rations came a small packet with matches, gum, toilet paper, salt and pepper, instant coffee, powdered creamer, and sugar. I ripped two matches out from the waterproof matchbook and carefully stuck one in the top of the freshly opened cake, like a candle on a birthday cake. I lit the second match to ignite the first. As the imitation candle flickered and slowly burned, I sang "Happy Birthday" to myself in a low voice, hoping not to draw any more attention than what the match may have done, while wrapped in my poncho liner under the cold, dark North Carolina sky.

As I ate my birthday cake alone, many uncontrollable thoughts ran through my head, mostly about how my now ex-girlfriend was with another man. The misery of not being able to contact her gave me a pain in the pit of my stomach. As I finished my private celebration with Carla on my mind, I contemplated why God allowed me to be so miserable when my intention was to search for a better way of life for the both of us, free and clear of the fear and intimidation that went along with my previous lifestyle. I questioned God and his motives, seeking answers to why my life had now taken such a miserable turn for what I considered to be the worse. Little did I know at the time that my future path had already been cleared before me by my own choices and that I was destined for a better quality of life.

I gazed into the deep, dark blue night at the millions of twinkling stars laid out across the Milky Way in blessed amazement of the heavenly show that performed before me. I uttered to God in a low voice, "If you really exist, then please give me a sign, something, anything. Just let me know you exist. Let me know everything is going to be alright and that I am going to be okay! Let me know that I am not alone and that you're watching over me."

As soon as the last word left my mouth, a bright shooting star with a long blue tail streaked across the night directly in front of me like a perfectly placed display of fireworks. I paused in astonishment but was still somewhat skeptical and simply considered it a coincidence. I tilted my head and looked back up into the night with my heart racing. I repeated my initial request, this time adding, "God, if that was really you giving me a sign, telling me that everything is going to be okay, then please do it again."

Again, the timing could not have been more perfect. Immediately, an exact replay of the first star flashed across the heavenly night, following the same path with its long blue tail. I had some difficulty at first accepting what I'd just seen but knew my request had been answered by God. At that point, I unconditionally felt and understood that I was no longer going to be alone; throughout my life, I would always have God's company. My belief in God was restored on this mysterious evening, and my prayers were answered.

Of course, I knew there were skeptics who would believe otherwise. But on that night, what was important to me was that my faith was restored and I became a true believer. I decided to keep my life-changing experience to myself. After an hour or so of shivering from the January cold while I digested what had happened, I collected myself and, with a smile of contentment, silently made my way back to the hut. Quietly and softly so as not to wake the other soldiers, I lay down on the now very cold steel bunk and, with a smile, closed my eyes for the first short night of sleep I'd had in many weeks.

I never saw or talked with Carla again. The last I heard was that she was married, had some children, and had sailed off into the sunset with her new husband happily ever after. She is now just a memory, a blink of time in my life; soon that life was going to change for me forever.

The eight months of grueling training seemed to fly by, and, before I knew it, graduation day was rapidly approaching. I asked my parents again if they'd attend the ceremony. I knew they would, of course, but how would they get to Fort Bragg? Although the financial aspect was a serious concern for Mom and Dad, there was an even bigger obstacle: my father's overwhelming fear of heights. Go figure; maybe that's where I inherited my own fear of heights.

Because of Dad's fear of flying, my parents needed to travel by train to North Carolina to watch their son proudly receive his diploma as one of America's best, a Green Beret. I enjoyed spending what little time I had available visiting with my parents, and I let them do some sightseeing while I processed out of training and into my new assignment.

They visited the Special Forces Museum, the Eighty-second Airborne Division Museum, and Fayetteville, but my Green Beret graduation was the main event they'd traveled thirteen hours to attend. The ceremony was a typical military ceremony, with the playing of the national anthem, a speech by the commander, the passing out of awards, and the presentation of the coveted Flash. The Flash was a representation of the unit that each graduating soldier was assigned, signifying that the soldier had successfully completed the arduous training and was now a fully qualified member of one of America's most elite. My assignment was to an A-Team with the Fifth Special Forces Group as an assistant team medic. I completed my training as a light weapons leader and waited to attend the Special Forces Medic Course. Each team member needed to be cross-trained in two separate specialties, such as demolitions, intelligence, communications, medical, or weapons.

As the auditorium slowly filled with soldiers, families, and friends, one could not help but notice the fatigue on the faces of the soon-to-be Green Berets. There was the obvious weight loss that revealed the tireless, demanding training, along with a sense of relief and accomplishment. The unyielding discipline and perseverance were evident as we sat quietly and patiently in our seats, waiting for the ceremony to begin. In true military fashion, the ceremony began like clockwork, with introductory comments followed by a brief history of the Green Beret and a roll call. The approximately one hundred new Green Berets approached the stage in alphabetical order.

As my name was called, I confidently walked onto the stage to receive my diploma and Flash. I exchanged a salute with the commander as my heart pounded inside my chest in nervous excitement. Walking off the stage, I cautiously glanced out the corner of my eye at the stairs so as not to fall and be a clumsy spectacle. I looked at my parents and could see the biggest and brightest smiles coming from them, as if they were saying, "That's my son!" Mom and Dad were ecstatic, thrilled to be part of this very special graduation day.

After the ceremony, we walked through the halls of the Special Forces headquarters, noting the pictures of all of the Congressional Medal of Honor recipients on the walls. We talked mostly about family and my new career, much like a normal family, which was a breath of fresh air for me. I felt no tension from my dad that day. It was a good day for me because I was able to communicate with him like a son with his father; but it was also a day of leisure after many months of demanding and exhausting training. I'd finally be able to sleep late for the first time in many months. More importantly, because of my parents' visit, I saw a glimmer of hope for my relationship with my dad.

Did my father finally let his selfish aspirations for my football career go and hope for something better for me? Had Dad been thinking about how he abused his family after I left for the service? Did he realize now that his son could easily be placed in a position of danger and that he might possibly lose him? What started the transformation?

The day went by extremely fast, and soon it was time for them to board the train and return to Rhode Island. I was elated that we'd shared a special moment together. They boarded the train and we said our good-byes; except for Dad, who always said, "So long!" We all had tears in our eyes, as though Dad were trying to tell me that he knew I'd done my best in football and that maybe it wasn't what God had planned for me. I never knew for sure, and that parting will always remain a mystery.

Over the next few years, I worked at becoming physically strong and absorbed as much technical and tactical information as possible, knowing that my life or a teammate's life might depend on that training one day. There came a point in my training where I felt confident that this was the right path for me. Football had been a team sport, much like the military. However, this was different.

Football and the army have very much in common; both are challenging physically and mentally and bring out the best or the worst in people. They also bring out the leadership qualities in certain persons.

Each move as a player had to be coordinated with prior practiced thought; each muscle and brainwave helped drive peak physical and mental performance as a single, continuous motion. In football, individual accomplishments, either good or bad, were noted by the senior leadership, coaching staff, or public, and the team depended on each player to achieve success or a win.

In the army, sweat during training in peacetime could mean less bloodshed in wartime, especially when your life depended not only on yourself but on your fellow soldier. There were no ifs, ands, or buts about it. The bottom line was that no matter how good a leader you were and no matter how good your soldiers were, the team was only as strong as its weakest soldier. The eyes of God are upon you.

My training on the A-Team as a medic inspired my interest to pursue a career in the field of medicine. I participated in several field-training missions, both at home and overseas, all of which heightened my appetite for medicine, especially for the many lower-extremity injuries the senior team medic and I treated. The ankle sprains, fractures, and skin diseases opened my eyes to a new and promising career.

I began to see opportunities knocking for me in medicine and peered into the possibility of becoming a physician, although I had great hurdles to leap in order to get to my goal. My short career as an enlisted soldier was certainly life-changing, lasting approximately thirty-nine months. An expiration of term of service (ETS) was the time when a soldier decided to reenlist, extend his or her contract, or simply go home to finish his or her remaining inactive reserve time. My ETS was rapidly approaching, and I awaited my final set of orders. Had I achieved all my goals, past and present? I was confident that I could have a very successful career as an enlisted soldier and a solid life in the military as well. Nevertheless, did I want to go that route?

Although the military offered unlimited opportunities, did I want to restrain my learning to what the military had to offer, and miss out on what the rest of the world might present to me? I understood that my military service would eventually end, as with everything, and decided to seek a civilian medical career. There was a long, hard road ahead of me, but my determination drove me to complete some things back home that I'd left unfinished, namely my education. I had nowhere to go but back home to Rhode Island, and nothing to do but make another attempt at college. This time I had medical school in my sights. Or was it just wishful thinking again?

I wanted to return home feeling that I was respected by my dad as a man, a man with genuine qualities. I was returning home not as an army hero but as a mature man with substance, a sound mind, and good character. In my heart and in good conscience, I knew I had exhausted every attempt at everything possible to make that a reality to my family. I watched with jealousy and envy as many of my fellow soldiers received warm fatherly embraces during family visits. Would I, at last, receive the same reception from my family or my father? I knew I wasn't getting any younger, but I was in the prime of my life. If I didn't set things straight for myself right now and get on a path to success, then when would I? I might never have another opportunity.

Still, many questions lurked in the back of my mind as I made plans to return home. Was my homecoming the prelude to another confrontation? Or would I be well received because of my merits and many accomplishments?

One thing I knew in my heart: I could never predict my father's behavior.

At least now I could control my own.

Chapter 7: *Big Man on Campus (Again!)*

The only place where success comes before work is in the dictionary.

~ Vince Lombardi

There was no doubt in my mind that joining the military and completing all the training made a rapid and drastic change in my life and certainly for my betterment. I found my new life's purpose, and the military guided me in the right direction, enabling me to understand that I had the potential to become successful at whatever I undertook. As I looked back over my extensive and arduous three-year army commitment, I realized that it provided me with a great sense of pride, instilled unbreakable confidence, and produced meaningful accomplishments. My tour of active duty left me with a positive outlook on life and taught me that I had the ability to look forward to a more promising future that held the key to a better and more rewarding life.

After receiving my discharge orders from Uncle Sam, I packed the few possessions I had and set my sights on going back to Rhode Island and my new adventure. It was an emotional day outside the team room at Fort Bragg as I said my good-byes to my teammates. These were men I'd trusted with my life. I had an eerie feeling, as though I were abandoning my brothers, and found it extremely difficult to leave.

As I walked to my car and looked back one last time, I began to rethink my future endeavors and what lay ahead of me beyond the gates of Fort Bragg. I started the engine, readying myself for the long fifteen-hour drive home, filled with a sudden, overwhelming sense of insecurity. I felt as if I'd lost my best friend or my soul mate and that an evil, anal being was grinding away at me, like a bad case of flaming hemorrhoids. I was leaving behind a regimented world where everything was preplanned: what uniform to wear; the training schedule for the next year; the time of breakfast, lunch, and dinner; and even the time for exercise. I was now on my own, with nobody telling me what to do or where to go; I was completely responsible only for myself. There was no more leadership, mentorship, camaraderie, or regimentation.

I was leaving a very structured world that had been very good to me and reentering a world that had been unkind. It felt like a reverse homecoming; I wanted to feel relief and euphoria at leaving the military behind, but instead I felt just the opposite. Seeing my father again felt as intimidating as my very first day at boot camp!

Many questions went through my head during that long, lonely drive home. Was I really about to do this? It was no little decision I was making here. It involved several more years of education and tens of thousands of dollars in tuition, all to be invested before I even made a single buck in return! How was I going to pay for school? I had the GI Bill, but that would pay only a portion of the expenses. Where would I live, and what was I going to do for work as a student? I had plenty of time to think. As I approached my parents' home at the end of the drive, however, I felt as if I'd answered all my questions.

The rebirthing process was not painless, but it was extremely gratifying. In addition to my own family, I welcomed my new family as an army veteran. I was deeply grateful for the opportunity to serve my country and fully understood the debt I owed to those who had honorably served before me. I was now a member of the club, so to speak. I recognized that my opportunities and future were a direct result not only of my hard work but also someone else's ultimate sacrifice for our freedom. Active duty cleared a path on the road that allowed me to regain my self-respect and helped me become a new, more responsible, and mature person.

When I had a few moments to reflect on my past, as I often did, I relived the conversation I'd had with my dad at the kitchen table almost four years earlier. That specific conversation sent a cold chill through my body as I remembered how he thought I'd never last a week through basic training. What echoed the loudest in my mind, however, were the questions

I was beginning to ask myself about what my father's intentions had been all along.

Had my father's comments been made to motivate me and encourage drive and determination, in the hopes I'd become a better man? On the other hand, had he been considering taking bets at the local bar that his son would be voted "The Man Most Likely *Not* to Succeed"? It troubled me to know that after all we'd been through, my dad might still not believe I was a real man.

Even as an adult, I wondered how long I'd have to fight for my father's approval. Was it something to strive for, or was it like my pro-football career, something better left in my pile of unfulfilled wishes and unrealized dreams? Was it time just to let go?

During my various specialty schools in the military, infantry, airborne, sniper, and Special Forces, it had been easy to keep my mind off Dad. As a member of a Green Beret A-Team, there were other important men with whom bonding was a priority. Every team member's life could one day depend heavily on another's skill and training. In some cases, you were much better off being lucky than good, although each team member would put his own life on the line for another.

These men were sincere and truly had every team member's best interest at heart. They were not ordinary men; they were hard men with intelligence, powerful wills, strong bodies, and genuine hearts. They were also fair men, men of conviction, who were fierce as well as fiercely loyal. They expected nothing less than superior results, and, when they got them, they responded accordingly. These men understood the meaning of unconditional love for their fellow soldier, but any Special Forces soldier would rather call it unconditional *respect*.

As a member of a close-knit military family, I had been welcomed with strong and forceful but open arms. As long as I held up my end of the bargain, everyone else respectfully contributed the same; they were like my brothers. Fail and falter though I might, there was always someone ready to lend a hand, help me to my feet, and give me another chance. It was such a refreshing change from my own home, where love was neither unconditional nor easy to come by.

The road to becoming one of America's mostly highly trained soldiers awakened my determination and pride. My initial Green Beret training as a light weapons expert opened the door to a new level of teamwork, cohesiveness, and leadership, but it was the cross-training in a second skill on the team as a medic that whetted my appetite for medicine—and all because of one good soldier.

The senior team medic, SSG Dave Williamson, was my mentor. He worked diligently and tirelessly to train me as the team's assistant medic. He spent hours and even days teaching me a plethora of medical and surgical techniques. Dave knew that the techniques he taught me could help save lives later on the battlefield, especially those of our fellow team members. In that regard, I was a willing pupil, and SSG Williamson knew that the more I learned, the better off the team would be in combat. It was apparent that the more I was taught, the more anxious I became to learn more about every aspect of the field of medicine. I was confident that I was going to be ready to aid our small band of brothers if I ever had to use my newly acquired aptitude.

The medical skills that SSG Williamson taught me actually saved my life one cool sunny Sunday afternoon. I'd started taking a new antibiotic for a throat infection and developed a severe allergic reaction called anaphylaxis. This type of allergic reaction can be deadly if it's not treated immediately. Within minutes after taking the antibiotic pill, my eyes and throat began to swell. Red swollen blotches began to quickly cover my entire body and face, and I had difficulty breathing. Wheezing sounds came from deep within my chest, making me nervous, but I maintained control and didn't panic, despite possibly being minutes away from death.

Having been taught a special set of skills, I was able to keep control of any situation, no matter how dire, and to remain calm and never panic. I knew something was going seriously wrong but maintained my composure, despite the fact that I knew I needed to get medical help quickly. I had more trust in SSG Williamson than I did in any emergency room doctors, so I called him, gasping for air, and desperately asked for help. Without hesitation, SSG Williamson jumped into his car with his medical aid bag. Within minutes, he rushed through the door of the trailer home I was renting.

SSG Williamson evaluated me and immediately recognized the signs and symptoms of anaphylaxis. He knew that his fellow team member, Sergeant John Gouin, was about to go into shock and possibly die if he wasn't treated immediately. In the true style of a Special Forces medic, he took control of the situation, evaluated the patient, and dispensed the appropriate injections of medication to reverse the rapid progression of the allergic reaction. Minutes after he administered the injections, I began to breathe easier. The wheezing ceased, and I soon became sleepy from the antihistamine, Benadryl, one of the drugs SSG Williamson had dispensed to reverse the reaction. Before I fell asleep, I groggily thanked him for saving my life as he continued to monitor my recovery.

There were no medals, citations, or awards given to SSG Williamson, which is very common; most Special Forces soldiers are unsung heroes. There was only the extreme debt of gratitude and gratefulness that I, his teammate, had for saving my life. There was no greater reward than saving a life, regardless of the conditions, and I couldn't praise Doc Williamson enough for his quick thinking. I recovered from the episode uneventfully, and the incident reinforced my desire for medicine. This was my first real-life experience as a medic; unfortunately, I was the patient, not the provider.

After that moment, which was followed by several training missions and a couple of overseas missions, I was further encouraged to pursue a career in the healthcare field. My insatiable appetite for a plethora of medical knowledge taught by Doc Williamson, whether it was practicing minor surgery or emergency medicine, was leading to an imminent career in medicine. Although I wasn't quite sure exactly what I specifically wanted to do in medicine, I was positive that my destiny lay before me. Thanks to SSG Williamson and my invaluable military training, I knew I was capable of completing any civilian medical training, no matter how difficult it appeared. Medicine was going to be a long, hard haul.

It was while I was on active duty that I seriously began contemplating exactly what to do in the field of medicine, not as a soldier but as a civilian. Thinking back to the many field exercises and overseas missions I'd undertaken as the assistant team medic, I remembered encountering and treating many foot and ankle problems. A neurosurgeon or family physician might have considered these injuries minor, because they sometimes appear to be nothing more than a sprained ankle, an infected ingrown toenail, or a metatarsal stress fracture. As insignificant as they seem to be, however, these problems could jeopardize the mission of an entire team, literally crippling the finest soldier and dangerously slowing down every member. The frequency of these injuries and the need for specialized treatments sparked my curiosity in the field of foot and ankle medicine and surgery.

I spent many months conducting due diligence and extensive research into a medical career focusing on the field of podiatry. This branch of medicine would allow me to provide quality medical care as a doctor, obtain a well-respected position in the community, and financially support a growing family. As a solo practitioner, I could plan flexible working hours and finally have a solid career.

The curriculum was only minimally different from that of traditional medical schools, but it was daunting nonetheless. After all, I still needed to finish my bachelor's degree, complete the Medical College Admission Test (MCAT), get accepted into a podiatry college, and complete another laborious four years of school, plus a two- or three-year residency at a hospital.

Only two months after I returned home from Fort Bragg, I re-enrolled at the university as a part-time student. I was a poor student the first time around as an athlete, and that placed me on a plateau, both emotionally and professionally. I felt I'd accomplished so much since then, yet I knew that if I didn't keep reaching, striving, and pushing myself, I'd fall into the familiar pattern of self-doubt. What could be worse than a rendezvous with the self-fulfilling prophecies of failure and disappointment?

The horizon was limitless, but, like a kid in a candy store, I had almost too many opportunities to choose from. Although I had started school again, I still waivered about whether I was doing the right thing. The army is a harsh and unyielding taskmaster, but a forgiving one. If you can make it to the highest levels, your future is almost certainly assured if you don't screw up. All you need to do is take that first step toward your destiny, like making that first parachute jump—there's no going back.

I decided to fill another of my life's blank pages: continue forward and obtain the academic credentials that had, until now, eluded me. I knew I wasn't dumb or a failure, as my father so often had suggested. In reality, I only lacked the effort needed to master the minefield of academics.

What was stopping me from getting that piece of paper that would open so many doors?

Nothing, it seemed! Clearly, I had the conviction to return to school and finish my bachelor's degree. However, I was haunted by one huge obstacle that prevented me from getting back into the university: my previously poor academic performance as a student athlete.

I was facing another crossroads. What would be the payoff for obtaining all this education? Which path should I choose: a very secure career in the military, or a civilian medical education? I knew exactly what path I wanted to follow, but doubt again shadowed me.

Little did anyone, including me, know that I was about to embark on a successful career as a foot and ankle surgeon along with a part-time army career after active duty. I continued as an officer in the Army Reserves and National Guard for over thirty years. Fate had intervened and paved an unexpected but exciting path to my future, with many twists and turns. The road to becoming a member of Special Forces led to the long-forgotten feelings of self-confidence, determination, and, above all, pride in knowing that I could accomplish anything if I applied myself.

In many ways, that initial tour was like a second chance at adulthood. I effectively wasted my first by fighting with my father, physically, emotionally, mentally, spiritually, and pretty much in every other way you might imagine. I knew I'd wasted so much time trying to please my father, appease my father, and, finally, hurt my father that I'd forgotten about taking care of myself.

In that sense, one could surmise that my dad was the ultimate victor. By putting him first and me second, I'd unwittingly bolstered my father's dominance. I'd been told by my dad so often what a failure I was, how horribly stupid, lazy, and worthless I was, that I literally had to retrain myself to believe in myself and regain my confidence in order to achieve my goals. Of course, I'd had some help, courtesy of Uncle Sam. Now, as a civilian, it seemed the horizon was limitless, curving endlessly through green pastures and open fields that I alone could decide to explore. I had been reborn in many ways.

Living back home in Rhode Island was a bittersweet time of reflection as I finally allowed myself to breathe from the constant training before assuming another challenge. It was sweet because of all that I'd accomplished in the rebuilding process, earning a second chance at adulthood. But it was bitter because of the sour aftertaste that Dad's passive-aggressive comments about my imminent failures had left in my mouth, still lingering over three years later.

My father felt I was making another mistake in leaving the army since I had accomplished so much in so little time. He lost faith in me, believing that I would never finish my college education. I desperately wanted to believe that when he chided me for leaving the army he'd just been administering his own brand of tough love. Nevertheless, I had mixed emotions and wondered if just the opposite were true. Had he secretly wanted me to fail all along?

My father's physical abuse might have been in the past, but his verbal abuse nonetheless caused internal bruising that I assumed would never quite fade. Even in this, my time of unqualified success, I still felt the sting of failure nipping at my heels.

Had I really succeeded, after all?

Was I eventually destined to return to active duty if I failed a second time in college?

On the other hand, was my dad correct? Was I just setting myself up for failure? So many different thoughts ran through my head, embedding so much confusion in my mind that I felt like I was standing in a sealed barrel and told to find the corner.

Chapter 8: *Rebuilding Burnt Bridges*

The significance of a man is not in what he attains but in what he longs to attain.

~ **Kahlil Gibran**

Like many college athletes, I had focused on parades, not grades, and failed to realize that my lack of academic effort would eventually come back to haunt me. Trying not to believe that the army was my sole backup plan, I set out to accomplish my task by setting reasonable and achievable goals with milestones attached. Aside from the fact that I'd previously ignored my education, I'd always understood that it was the keystone to a successful career, along with hard work and just plain, old-fashioned good luck.

Now I took that personal drive one step further and set my goals even higher. I didn't want just a college education; I wanted the pinnacle of a college education: a medical degree. The idea had been a mere pipe dream once upon a pre-army time, but perhaps it was my elite military training that drove me to seek advanced medical training now. I knew I didn't want to be a neurosurgeon or a cardiologist; rather, I was interested in podiatry thanks to the many foot and ankle injuries I'd seen in the military. I aspired to achieve a degree as a foot and ankle surgeon and became a doctor of podiatric medicine.

Was I a late bloomer or just a wishful thinker in believing I could make it through medical school? The dream, despite my aspiration to become a physician, was slowly fading because of my prior poor grades. It was the ultimate case of rebuilding burnt bridges with half enough wood and twice as far to go!

How could I rebuild these bridges? Was there someone out there who believed in second chances who would give me a desperately needed opportunity? Where was I to turn? I started with the most experienced people, the educational counselors. After I encountered several of them at the university, they all suggested I pursue "another profession," or, as they so delicately recommended, attempt to finish my physical education degree. Reality set in, leaving me feeling deflated, desperate, and alone. Despite the setbacks, I tried to see myself as others saw me, not as a failed student athlete but as a mature, determined man looking for another chance at life.

Considering my academic record and my military accomplishments, it only made sense that they would encourage me to pursue my strengths and downplay my weaknesses. Standing in front of them, after all, was a man who seemed like a big, rough and tumble guy, adept at the battlefield, not the classroom.

It was obvious why they'd encourage me to finish my physical education degree. However, I wanted more than that. Couldn't they see? Didn't they understand that this was my opportunity for a fresh start? Did none of my recent successes matter to them? Could the admissions staff not separate my success in the military from my failure during my first time on campus? Wasn't that their job to recognize and nurture potential for the benefit of our society?

Regardless of how I was viewed by those small-minded counselors (although I couldn't really blame them for judging a book by its worn and tattered cover), I was determined not to give up. As a last-ditch effort, I asked to see the head of the department. There was only one option left, as far as I could see, which was to meet face to face with the dean of arts and sciences and convince him that I desperately needed a second chance at academics. I had a monumental task ahead of me, persuading the dean that I was mature, fully capable intellectually, and highly determined to achieve and maintain the grades that would win me admission into medical school.

There comes a time when you just have to be humble, and the day I met with the dean was one of those days. I nervously walked up to the dean's secretary, informing her who I was and that I had an appointment with the dean that afternoon. She stood up, walked to a majestic mahogany door, and slowly opened it for me. It certainly wasn't purposeful on the dean's part, but everything about the cavernous office made me feel very small. The heavily lined bookshelves and antique furniture didn't ease the anxiety very much.

As I wearily yet confidently walked across the office, I politely reached out with my right hand and introduced myself to the dean. I sat directly in front of him and maintained as much eye contact as possible. The slightly graying, handsome dean was not intimidating at all as a person and had a sincere personality. I was hoping I'd be able to communicate a sense of determination along with an air of confidence without presenting myself as too cocky. Then it hit me like a sledgehammer: my entire future depended on the decision of this one man, but he was just another man, a man who could determine my fate with the stroke of a pen. I couldn't believe that I'd ever again feel as helpless and meek as I did that day.

As I sat down in front of his desk, conflicting thoughts raced through my mind, and I began to question whether I really should be here begging for an opportunity from someone who put his pants on the same way everyone else did. I was not in the habit of conceding my fate to others; it was an extremely humbling experience. Nonetheless, I intently watched the dean flip through the pages of my previous transcripts. When he stopped flipping through the pages, he peeked over the rim of his reading glasses.

Cold apprehension flashed through my body as I observed some disturbing movements coming from his eyes. The dean seemed to have discovered something in the transcripts that was not very reassuring. Immediately I thought the worst and could see the tragic end coming like the falling blade on a razor-sharp guillotine.

Furthermore, I was beginning to see a career as an infantry soldier in the army, my backup plan. As expected, he looked dead into my anxious eyes and flatly suggested that I pursue "another curriculum." I was emotionally crushed, but, hat in hand, I once again blurted out a plea: "There must be some way I can start over? Please, sir, I need a second chance. I can do this. Please?" Until that day, I'd begged only one other man in my entire life, but this time I placed my pride elsewhere in order to convince the dean that I was completely sincere and determined to achieve my goal.

After approximately thirty minutes of discussion and continued pleading by me, the dean finally came up with a plan. He looked directly at me with a poker face and politely suggested that if I could maintain a 3.3 GPA for the next two semesters as a full-time student, he would reconsider my readmission into the college and delete any failing grades and incompletes. Additionally, he would make all the previous entries on my record, regardless of grade, into "Pass," thus beginning a new grade point average.

I was ecstatic, to say the least, and was so excited that I had to pause for a moment to digest what had happened. I was actually being given an opportunity to start anew, something that came along once in a lifetime. It was a godsend. I stood up and, with my sweaty palm, grasped the dean's hand, shaking it with ecstatic gratitude and sincere thankfulness.

"I cannot thank you enough, and I will prove to you that I can do this. Thank you again so much! Thank you, thank you!" I repeated to him.

I was elated and determined to meet the dean's requirements; I wasn't about to pass this up. It was going to be a long, hard road, but I was finally back in control and in charge of my destiny. Again, my head and eyes were directed forward. I was going to complete my bachelor's degree and move on to medical school, eventually graduating as a doctor of podiatric medicine.

Since I'd already wasted a full football scholarship, I felt a sense of responsibility to pay for school this time on my own. Student loans and the GI Bill were the major source of financial support during my collegiate endeavor. I declined other financial assistance, including an ROTC scholarship, though I accepted a couple hundred dollars here and there from my mother to keep me going. Her unyielding determination and moral support for her son moved me in the right direction and, in the end, encouraged me to complete my entire education. My dad, on the other hand, never thought I'd finish a week of basic training, so what would make him think I could ever finish medical school? He conveyed an attitude that his son would not have one iota of a chance of getting accepted into medical school, never mind the idea that he'd finish.

Whenever my father and I talked during those years, occasions that were infrequent and awkward, I would purposefully shy away from any conversation regarding my attendance in school. True to form, Dad discussed my attempt at medical school with his friends several times at the local bar and said I would "never make it through to graduation."

I was more determined than ever to make it through school. The blinders came on, the sleeves were rolled up, and the head went down. I was locked on the target—a medical degree—like a heat-seeking missile. I worked diligently and met the requirements for the first two semesters as agreed. The dean kept his promise to reset my GPA and transcripts. The hard work and the unwillingness to fail are what got me accepted into the premed program.

As I rolled through the spring semester with a 3.3 GPA, I earned some extra money as a bartender. I found a great little bar nestled away on a small beach at the southern end of the Rhode Island coast. A few of my friends had been working as bartenders, and I thought back to those grim and nervous days at the club. I had some concerns about possibly getting back into the same rut, but I knew this time I could keep the blinders on and stay focused on my ultimate goal.

After having a few beers with the manager of the beach bar, he offered me a job as a bartender, and I didn't even have to get into a fight to get it. I accepted the position for the summer. It was very difficult to take this position, considering the extremely daunting working conditions involving bikinis, beaches, and babes, but I knew someone had to do it, so why not me? What could be better than working a great job at a prime oceanfront bar on the Atlantic Ocean, especially during the summer? It was the perfect workplace for a single guy in his late twenties who was in the prime physical condition of his life.

Early one summer evening, a warm ocean breeze was blowing through the windows in the bar, and the smell of the salt air mixed with the sound of the crashing waves on the shoreline, all setting the tone for this busy little New England seaside town. The jukebox was blaring "Start Me Up" by the Rolling Stones, while customers and tourists sat around the bar in their beach attire with sun-reddened bodies smelling of suntan lotion. A man casually walked up to the bar and sat on one of the stools directly in front of me. Oddly enough, I felt an immediate connection with the man, despite never having laid eyes on him before.

It was the strangest feeling, a feeling that maybe only the Special Operations community understands; they can detect one another thanks to a certain recognizable kinship. I was wearing one of my Special Forces T-shirts. This gruff-looking man decided to ask me a question. He had short, graying hair, a full salt-and-pepper moustache, and a stubby, unshaven face. The man took a sip from his beer and in a sarcastic way sighed and said to me, "Are you a Special Forces guy?"

I replied, "Well, I was a few months ago. Just got off active duty."

The man responded, "Once an SF guy, always an SF guy! It never leaves your blood." I knew immediately that this man had to be a Special Forces soldier and asked him the same question in return. "Are you?"

He didn't respond immediately. Instead, he introduced himself as Tom. He said he was still on active duty teaching as an ROTC instructor at the same university I was attending, the University of Rhode Island. He was a master sergeant with several tours in Vietnam under his belt, full of experience and vast amounts of training.

He finally responded after a few sips of beer, "Yes, I was with the 10th SF Group." Immediately the war stories started to fly back and forth, as if we'd known each other for years and years. We discovered that we were brothers and felt the sacred bond. I was on the money when Tom told me he was Special Forces-qualified.

We traded war stories for the next hour as I continued to work my shift at the bar. Then Tom asked me if I'd ever thought about becoming an officer, a dreadful thought as an enlisted man. The nerve of this master sergeant! I sarcastically laughed and flatly declined. I insisted that I wasn't officer material. Tom asserted that I had plenty of experience and that I'd make it easily through the curriculum. He said I should look into joining the ROTC program.

Reluctant to veer from my goal of medical school, I declined with a polite but forceful, "No, thank you."

Tom was not pushy and said to me, "If you join the program, you'd enter as an advanced cadet and only have to complete two years." He added, "You shouldn't have any problems making it through the program, with honors." Tom was assuming I'd succeed since I'd already received most of the same training as a Special Forces sergeant. "In fact," he concluded, "you'll probably be selected as the student battalion commander after you complete your first year."

I put some serious thought into becoming an army officer over the next several days, and eventually it started to sound like a good idea. I decided that if I wasn't accepted into medical school then at least I should have a backup plan to go back into the military as an officer. The pay was good, the respect was good, and the responsibility was immense.

Later that week, I made an unannounced visit to the ROTC department to see Tom. He was in his uniform, and he was now Master Sergeant Thompson with specialty tabs and qualification badges everywhere. It was obvious that MSG Thompson had served in combat during the Vietnam War and was highly decorated. He'd completed more than twenty years of service and appeared to most soldiers as a "man's man." I envied Tom for his successful military career but also looked at him as possibly my new mentor.

Tom was someone who had the capability and experience to hone my leadership skills and make me into an outstanding and exemplary officer if I chose that path. We walked the halls of the department; MSG Thompson introduced me to the passing cadre and showed me around the ROTC office. I was filled with skepticism, not thoroughly convinced that I wanted to be an army officer.

The attitude and enthusiasm on the university campus was so different from when I attended the first time during the early 1970s, the Vietnam War era. I remembered walking past the ROTC department in my football uniform, seeing students who were dressed in the style of the era, including long hair, plaid bell-bottom pants, and paisley shirts, carrying banners and posters protesting the war.

The ROTC program had few participants, no more than fifteen in the entire class. In retrospect, they deserved much credit for standing by their desire and determination to become army officers at an undesirable time for the military in America. Even then, I thought it was okay to disagree with the policies and makers of war but not to condemn the young, brave warriors who gave us the right to enjoy our freedom of speech.

Tom had rekindled my desire to be in uniform and get back into the military mind-set, and I decided to join the ROTC program. Since I had more than three years of excellent and rigorous enlisted military training, I was placed in the advanced status and was required to complete only the final two years of the program, exactly as Tom said. I was thrilled and couldn't believe my good fortune. Thanks to one spontaneous meeting at a Rhode Island bar, I was now on my way to becoming an army officer and, ultimately, a physician.

My natural leadership ability surfaced, and, with my experience, I quickly emerged as a mentor among my own classmates. I wasn't competitive but was fully capable of teaching and easily volunteered to share with my classmates whatever knowledge I possessed. This was an obvious sign to the cadre that Cadet Gouin's potential as an officer was unlimited. The student battalion commander's position was prestigious and highly desired by most of the cadets. Yet this position also brought a higher level of responsibility, and selection, based on merit, academics, and leadership, was made by all members of the university program. My fellow cadets and cadre voted me to fill the rank as the cadet battalion commander because of my stellar performance during my first year. The prophecy of MSG Thompson appeared to be coming to fruition. He could not have been more correct in his initial assumption and assessment regarding my capabilities and my future development as an officer.

I entered my second year as an advanced ROTC student, which really made me a senior cadet; but as a civilian student, I was still a junior. Regardless of my station as a student, everything was going according to plan. I graduated second in the entire class of cadets at ROTC Advanced Camp, my old stomping grounds at Fort Bragg. I received several awards, including The Association of the United States Army Medal, which was pinned on by none other than John O. Marsh, then the secretary of the army; the Superior Cadet Award, the highest award for a cadet; and the Physical Fitness Proficiency Ribbon. I also received high military honors as a Distinguished Military Graduate from the University of Rhode Island.

Commissioning day as a second lieutenant rapidly approached, and a newly acquired responsibility was soon to come with it. The tides had finally turned, and I had been transformed from an enlisted soldier into an officer. My focus now, besides medical school, was aimed at taking care of the very soldier that I'd epitomized just a few short years ago. I was a loyal and dedicated Special Forces sergeant who'd never dreamed of becoming an officer in the United States Army.

Proud of my accomplishments, I requested that my parents pin on my newly achieved gold lieutenant rank, better known in the military as "Butter Bars." This military ceremony was another familiar, all-family affair; after all, they'd attended my basic training graduation at Fort Dix, New Jersey, as well as my graduation from Special Forces training at Fort Bragg. Having them present at my commissioning ceremony was an important part of my achievement, as well as yet another opportunity to appease my dad.

Deciphering the expression in my father's eyes, which were free from their usual glassy barroom appearance, I decided that Dad was finally coming to terms with the fact that his son would no longer accept failure as an option. Despite the hardships and disappointments, I pushed and pushed myself to succeed, continually proving to my father that I was not a failure, which was a lifelong task for me. The insatiable urge to give my father more of that sense of pride in his son only opened more doors for me. I was accomplishing things that most uneducated fathers dream of, not only for themselves but also for their children. Providing opportunities for their children is the greatest gift parents can give.

It seemed like it was basic training all over again, only this time I had much more riding on my academic success. As my undergraduate years flew by, however, my dad seemed to mellow—especially after one final confrontation, a confrontation that was to change our relationship forever.

The University of Rhode Island was only an hour or so from my parents' home, so quick trips to see them were frequent. When I was visiting them at their home one Saturday evening with my beach-bar girlfriend, Dad stumbled through the door in his typical fashion, smelling of smoke and alcohol. He had the usual red, glazed-over eyes. He sat at the table with everyone, and it was only a matter of minutes before he started in with his condescending comments about me and my attendance at school. I was embarrassed in front of my new girlfriend. At this point, I was too mature, and this kind of behavior was no longer acceptable, no matter whose home I was visiting. As his rude comments continued, I looked at my girlfriend and said, "Let's go. I don't need this, nor do you need to see any of this!"

As I stood up and began to calmly walk out of my father's home, he blurted out, "That's typical. It's just like you to run!" What Dad was referring to was a childhood incident that happened to me when I was twelve years old. As I was walking back from school alone late one afternoon, I was approached by two fifteen-year-old boys who were much bigger and stronger than I was and who were just looking for a reason to rough someone up. They were typical neighborhood bullies. Sure enough, they approached me. After making a few intimidating comments, one proceeded to grab me, while the other one beat me viciously. Although I was used to getting beat up by someone larger and more powerful, I struggled to free myself and looked for the quickest way out. The usual response at that age is to run, and I did. Not having the strength or the size to defend myself against two larger boys, I chose the flight response.

It was crucial for my own protection that I got home as quickly as possible, cleaned up any blood on my face, and tried to hide any torn clothes before my father got home. If Dad knew that I hadn't fought back and that I ran instead of defending myself, there would be more hell to pay, and another beating would be imminent.

As I walked around the corner from the back of the foundry across the street, there sat my father's car, parked directly in front of the apartment. As I wiped the blood off my lip, I gulped and then sighed deeply and mentally prepared myself to face my dad for a second round of one-sided sparring. The hair on my neck rose straight up, and a chill went down my spine as I crept toward the front steps of the apartment. I stood tall and was ready to accept my fate. Something ugly was about to happen, and I was sure I was going to be on the receiving end. Walking through the front door and making instant eye contact with my dad was unavoidable, especially since he was sitting in his favorite chair. There was no way for me to walk past my father to get to the bathroom to clean up.

My father took one look at me and said, "What happened to you?"

Naively assuming that my dad would have some sympathy for me, I replied, "These two guys, about fifteen or sixteen years old, jumped me and beat me up behind the foundry on the railroad tracks!"

Dad immediately asked, "What did you do to them?"

I responded in my usual low, subordinate voice, "Nothing. I just ran!"

"You did what?" he bellowed. "You don't mean to tell me that you didn't defend yourself? You're a sissy! No man in this house is going to be a sissy and run from anybody!"

I received two beatings that fateful day, one from the neighborhood bullies and the other from my dad. I would have preferred the two bullies all over again instead of my dad. After my second beating that day, I made a vow never to back down or be pushed around ever again, not by anyone, either as a child or as an adult.

However, my brother, Michael, who was fifteen years old, was not about to let two beatings happen to his little brother without someone answering to him; of course, our dad was definitely excluded. Michael was taller and more slender than I was, with broader shoulders, and was equally used to getting beatings from our father.

One Saturday evening, Michael was caught lying to Dad when he was spotted smoking a cigarette. Michael denied it, but somebody else had seen him smoking earlier in the day and reported what they'd seen to Dad. Of course, our Dad didn't tolerate cigarettes, but lying to him and getting caught brought the most severe form of punishment. Dad looked Michael straight in the eye and asked him about the cigarette. Michael flat-out denied it, which was a serious mistake. Did it really matter? He knew the beating was coming regardless of how he responded.

Then it happened: the sound of an open hand against a tender youthful face. *Whack!* Michael was stunned and fell to the floor. Dad helped him to his feet and said, "Don't you lie to me!"

Dad picked him up off the ground and tossed him across the room into a recliner. Michael tumbled face first into the chair, and the force pushed the chair over backward, with him in it. He was semiconscious at that point, and I decided to stay clear of my father's wrath. Dad pounced on Michael as if he were a punching bag hanging from the ceiling. To this day, Michael still smokes cigarettes, probably more in defiance of our father than because of a physical addiction.

As a matter of coincidence, a few days later, as Mike was doing errands for Mom at a local market, he literally ran into one of the boys who'd beaten me. Mike proceeded to return the undesirable favor. It happened right in the neighborhood grocery store, with cans and other items falling off the shelves as Mike jacked the boy up against the shelving filled with canned goods. Mike promised to me that he'd beat their asses even more severely if they ever came close to his little brother again. When I found out the news, I was so excited that someone had finally been on my side and, even more so, that it was my big brother.

As I walked out the front door and into the yard, my father's comment hit home, and I replied, "At least I'm not a damn drunk!" My girlfriend and I continued to my car when we heard some commotion coming from inside the house.

A thunderous noise could be heard as Dad came running down the front stairs after me. Everyone in the house followed him outside, calling his name and repeatedly asking him to calm down. They froze as Dad forcefully approached me like a bull chasing a matador, thinking he would put me on the run. But then, right there in Dad's own front yard, with everyone watching, I stopped, turned, and, with the same hateful reddened glazed look my father had, came nose to nose with my dad. My father abruptly stopped his charge and seemed surprised that I was not backing down.

He expected me to run, but I stood my ground as I had vowed I would as a child. I leaned slightly forward into Dad's personal space, looked him right in the eye, and said, "Just blink and I will take your damn head off! Go on, just do it, give me an excuse!" Dad paused, gulped, and stood there in total shock. At that moment, Dad was slapped in the face by the fact that he knew his son had been highly trained to kill, was good at what he did, and could actually follow through with what he had threatened.

Looking directly into my father's eyes without blinking, I paused a moment to let Dad respond, but he remained silent. Then I said, "Just what I thought!"

Dad could no longer use his bully tactics. He knew his family was watching the confrontation and now feared for their safety. My family saw a bigger dog emerge in the pack, and Dad put his tail between his legs.

Then I turned my back on my father and walked away.

Things were about to change and change, eventually, for the better. I didn't know if it was my dad's age, exactly, or that he was just getting tired of lording the advantage over me, but whatever it was, he must have come to terms with the fact that his son was no longer going to stand by and accept the abuse he'd dished out for so many years. It was no longer going to happen, not to me and definitely not to my mother!

I was going to make something of myself without my father's negative reinforcement or approval. I was ready to make a difference in my life and applied for admission to several podiatry schools. I was confident I'd be accepted, complete the courses, and ultimately receive my degree.

My mother was always supportive of my goal to enter medical school, despite Dad's usual negative comments. It was her faith in God that kept her strong and devoted to Catholicism; she was a faithful believer in Jesus Christ and all the saints, with their abilities to intercede on a person's behalf in troubled times. Mom was very partial to one particular saint, St. Jude, the saint of the impossible, who had a close relationship with Jesus.

For many years, she would pray from a small prayer card, asking St. Jude to guide me through the educational process successfully. She would pray this novena for me daily, hoping that I'd have the determination and drive to make it through school and become a successful physician.

My due diligence paid off. Eventually I was accepted into several podiatry schools, but my final choice was the school in Chicago. It must have been fate;

the original St. Jude shrine is located in South Chicago. My new apartment, in the near north side of Chicago, was only a few blocks from the college, but it was a significant distance from the shrine.

One blustery Saturday morning in December, after attending school for several months and becoming familiar with the city, I decided to get up early to visit the shrine. I was used to the cold from growing up in Rhode Island, but this kind of cold was miserable, especially with a wind that traveled right through you. It took me some time to make the adjustment.

I felt a compelling urge to take a trip to the shrine that day just to light a candle and say a prayer of thanks for my mother. I was hoping that when I got there I could purchase a small statue as a Christmas gift for her with a little extra money I'd saved.

The journey required several transfers on the El to get to the South Side; then I had to walk several blocks past some housing projects and through some low-income areas. I was familiar with these areas since I'd grown up in a housing project; I was street smart, with enough common sense to know when and where to walk.

Although there is a fine line between streets smarts, bravery, and stupidity, I knew exactly how to handle myself in areas like this. The apartment complex where I lived was just on the other side of the El from Chicago's worst housing project, Cabrini Green. I would walk past the El to a local fried chicken restaurant that was in an area where most white men would not think of going. I made several trips to this restaurant and never really encountered any problems, although occasionally I heard, "Hey! What you doing in here, white boy?"

I replied with a grin, "Same thing as you, buying some chicken." My street smarts told me that if I showed any fear whatsoever I wouldn't have a good time. Lesson number one in the housing project: never let them know you're afraid of anything.

I heard that same man say, "Crazy white boy!" No further comments were necessary from me. I knew just what to say and when to say it, and I knew when to leave well enough alone. Otherwise, a small problem could escalate into a much bigger one.

In any event, I'd finally made it to the shrine despite getting temporarily disoriented a few times along the way. I walked up to the front of the small red brick church, which didn't seem fancy from the outside. There was very little stained glass on the front. It had a shiny bronze dome with a crucifix centered on the crest. There was nothing impressive about the tarnished copper doors. There wasn't anything majestic about it physically, but it was awe-inspiring just the same. Walking into this monument of hope was an exhilarating experience. As I entered this simple, quiet, and peaceful church, I immediately detected the aroma of burning candles, which filled the church with an air of sacredness. Burning in the shrine were hundreds of lighted candles that flickered and sparkled with hopeful intentions for someone's improved health, improved financial situation, or strengthened personal relationship.

The warmth of the church filled me, and contentment overwhelmed me as I heard the sound of each footstep echoing off the marble floors as I walked past the old oak pews. Humbly, I approached the altar of St. Jude, which lay just to the right of the sanctuary. Under the marble altar there was a large frame that encompassed a glass casing; thousands of letters and requests were stacked inside like thousands of dollar bills in a bank vault.

I sat around for a while and prayed not only for my successful completion of school but also for my mother, wishing for her a healthier and better way of life. I walked into the small shop that had many different kinds of statuettes and other assorted religious items. As I browsed, I found the perfect statuette of St. Jude, measuring about a foot tall, wrapped in a red and green robe and carrying a staff in his left hand. At the base of the statuette was a placeholder for a votive candle. It was the perfect Christmas present to bring to my mother.

My mother's vigilant prayers, combined with my hard work over the next four years in school, proved rewarding for Dad, but he was beginning to feel like he needed to eat his words. Being accepted into and completing podiatry school was something my dad never thought would happen. In fact, Dad had mentioned to only a few of his close friends at the bar that his son was in podiatry school; he feared being a laughingstock if I failed.

I completed podiatry school, maybe not the first in my class but definitely not the last. When graduation day eventually rolled around, Dad knew he was going to have to fly for the first time to see his son accept his diploma. Although my family had purchased airline tickets, it was only on the day before the celebration that my dad had actually made up his mind that he was going to Chicago to attend my graduation ceremony and was going to do it by plane. He had never flown in his life, and I was duly impressed that he would take that frightful, white-knuckled step onto an airplane to visit me. It healed some of the lingering wounds. I knew my father had gone way out of his comfort zone.

Best of all, I was sure my father actually did it to please me and to finally add to his bragging rights regarding his son's recent success. On graduation day, it was a sight to behold: there was my father, dressed in a dark blue sport coat and tie to match, his chest out proudly, seated as close to the stage as possible to watch his son receive his doctorate of podiatric medicine diploma.

Maybe there was a hopeful, bright, and promising future as father and son for us after all.

Chapter 9: *The Best Man*

It is for us to make the efforts. The rest is always in God's hands.

~ **M. K. Gandhi**

My life from adolescence to adulthood was filled with a blend of happenstance, good karma, and roll-up-your-sleeves hard work. I was fortunate enough to turn the correct corners at the right times and clearly recognize the best opportunities that were waiting for me, like it or not. As my sister Carol often reiterated to our family and me, "John is one of those fortunate individuals who could fall into a bucket of 'poop' and come out smelling like a rose."

Along the way, my gut instinct and good fortune helped me make the correct decisions that ultimately affected my future. It was a twist of fate that I created a life for myself which otherwise might not have existed. Had I followed the straight and narrow path, not stumbled down a darkened alley, or taken the road less traveled a time or two, things could have been very different.

As the natural sequence of events unfolded and my life continued on its course, completing my education became my top priority. Above all else, I was going to finish this endeavor on my own terms. I had made it this far under my own steam; no way was I going to look for handouts or lifts-up from anybody now. No matter how difficult, tight, lean, or sparse things got during this period in my life, I moved forward one step at a time under my own weight and on my own terms.

As obvious as it may seem, having girlfriends or dating, let alone finding a mate, was not very high on my list of short-term goals. If I met someone who was patient and not overly aggressive and fell passionately in love, then maybe there would be a future. As selfish as it may sound, my future was going to be on my terms and only after I finished school.

You never know when things will change and opportunity might knock, especially when it comes to sudden, surprising romance. In my case, I was in my last year of school, with only eight months remaining until graduation. The light at the end of the tunnel was staring me right in the face. To say I had my eyes on the prize would be the understatement of the year. The last thing, the *very* last thing, I needed, wanted, or could handle at that moment was a love interest. Naturally, as luck would have it, that's exactly what I got.

After attending a late lab one evening, a few of my classmates and I decided to go to a local bar for happy hour. Judy, the only woman in the group, had said that she had three new roommates and that she would certainly love to invite them out for a few drinks. "You'll like my new roommates; I promise you they are *very nice*," she remarked.

To her fellow classmates, Judy was more like one of the guys, especially in our little study group. She had the enviable combination of a slender figure, gorgeous aqua-blue eyes, and naturally thick jet-black hair. She was fun-loving but very industrious and studious; she took her education very seriously. She was also extremely intelligent.

Of course, being typical males, we asked if her friends were good-looking. She explained that her roommates were attractive, as they were all flight attendants. She said coolly and confidently, "They are all really very nice."

"Oh, we get it; they are 'really very nice,' huh?" I asked, joking with her. In guy-speak, "really very nice" was our clue that they were not very attractive at all. In this particular situation, the law of natural selection applied. Naturally, we reasoned, and, of course, we weren't very selective. If they were good-looking flight attendants, then what were they doing wanting to have a few drinks with podiatry students, right?

Sitting around in the bar, we looked like just any other group of guys on the prowl. However, far from being the archetypal campus lounge lizards, we had Judy on our side. Thinking the night was a sure thing with a few flight attendants, we all raised our glasses and toasted to some possible good fortune.

The night wore on, and the good fortune was slowly diminishing. From the looks of it, our so-called sure thing had quickly soured. Judy was usually prompt, but that night she was running a little late; we assumed we'd just been blown off. Being blown off by "very nice" flight attendants was not exactly on our very special things to do list.

Then, just as we finished getting the disappointed words out of our mouths, Judy came walking in with three drop-dead gorgeous women. "Very nice flight attendants" indeed! I felt my Adam's apple make quivering motions, and my chin dropped to my knees. I realized that we guys had been sadly mistaken in our prejudgments. (Maybe "really very nice" was Judy's personal colloquialism for "really very hot.")

Once Judy concluded the introductions and everyone was comfortable, I was quick on the draw, offering to buy the first round of drinks. Despite my typically cool, calm, and collected military demeanor, I was suddenly dumbfounded, beginning to stutter and rapidly losing my composure. I had never acted like this with any women in my life; then again, I figured, these were no regular women. They were knockouts, every one of them.

Standing out was a beautiful, blonde-haired Texan named Leslie. She had a personality no self-respecting author could avoid calling "bubbly" and a southern accent that would make any man, Confederate or Yankee, fall to his knees. Maybe it was that honey-dripping Texas accent that northern men love to hear or that southern charm that attracted me; whatever it was, she had my undivided attention.

That night was the beginning of a long relationship. Over the next eight months, Leslie and I were apart only when I was studying and she was flying or working. We seemed to be puzzle pieces that suddenly clicked, peas in a pod, pick your cliché; we connected instantly, spontaneously, and in a way that made it very, very hard to separate. We were together constantly, enjoying each other's company. Leslie wasn't pretentious and didn't require expensive dinners, fine jewelry, or the best shows. She was fully aware of my priorities and was not for a second going to interfere with my education. She accepted me for who I was and not what I was going to be. But I knew that with any woman there was a deep-seated need for security, whether it was financial, physical, or emotional. I was confident that Leslie felt in her heart that she accepted me simply as John, without conditions or disclaimers.

Though four years of school had seemed interminable, the last 240 days literally flew by, and graduation day rapidly approached. Of course, graduation day was anything but. I was not finished with school quite yet; I still had three more years of postgraduate training to complete. Although the largest hurdle, receiving my diploma, had officially been overcome, there was still the preceptorship and the two-year residency to tackle. It seemed as though I was forever *not* making any money. I was close to $100,000 in student loan debt, a reality that made my stomach churn with a constant dread, making it hard to sleep at night and even harder to get out of bed in the morning. How was I going to pay all that back and have some kind of a life at the end of the day?

It wasn't going to be easy. With Leslie firmly at my side, I started planning for the next phase of my life: a wife, a home, and a job. Leslie was patient with what we both referred to as my "podiatry poverty," despite occasionally hinting about our future together.

I was steadfast in refusing to commit; as I figured it, how was I supposed to have a wife, children, and home without a job, not to mention repay the school debt? I felt as though I had a responsibility to start married life with a clean slate. How could I ever ask Leslie to share my burden, let alone continue to wait patiently for me to finally turn a profit? Deep down, I knew it was my financial burden, and I was determined to eliminate it as quickly as possible.

"Finish everything first, and the rest will fall in place" reverberated in my mind and became my mantra. While I completed my residency, I started looking for a permanent home and visited several states as possible locations for opening a practice. I'd discussed with Leslie that I was tired of the Chicago cold and was interested in enjoying a warm or moderate climate. She deviously suggested with her southern charm that I might want to look at her home state of Texas to start a practice. (How convenient!)

Nevertheless, even a starving podiatry student like me knew there was a method to her madness. She subtly mentioned South Texas, especially Corpus Christi, where she spent her spring breaks every year. I was puzzled. After all, being from the North, I'd seen the television commercials and cowboy movies with deserts, rattlesnakes, tumbleweeds, and oil fields. Leslie's sultry spring breaks notwithstanding, Texas just didn't seem too tempting to me at the time. I was more interested in California or Florida, but I decided to take a trip, knowing I was required by the military to complete three months of training in the Officer Basic Course at Fort Sam Houston, Texas, upon residency completion.

Together we made a weekend trip to Corpus Christi, billed as "The

Sparkling City by the Sea," to see if I would enjoy living and practicing there. We'd been there for approximately twenty-four hours, gathering as many sights and as much demographic information as possible, when I knew I could forget all about Florida and California; this was the place where I would raise my family and start a practice.

The city had plenty of sunshine, warm sandy beaches, and, even better, palm trees, something I had always wanted swaying breezily in my front yard. Best of all, there was a lot of potential for this city to grow, and I could grow with it. Therefore, despite my earlier reservations, I started my initial planning for a life, home, and family in Corpus Christi, Texas.

Of course, that involved cutting some very close ties with my family back in Rhode Island, especially my mother and sister. Several times after graduation, my dad suggested that I return to Rhode Island and start my practice there; but, frankly, I understood the consequences of returning to my small hometown. I knew that if I returned to Rhode Island, my dad, with his dominating personality, would eventually try to run the practice and dictate what went on in my business, regardless of whether I wanted him to help or not. I hadn't come this far only to take a step backward and return to that cowering twelve-year-old boy who feared his father's return home from work every night. I was not about to let my father attempt to run my life again, and my father would have crept into doing that a little at a time.

That was *not* going to happen, especially with a new wife possibly in tow.

Over the next year, Leslie chose to move back to Texas because of job opportunities and relocated to the Dallas-Fort Worth airport. She was fortunate enough that she could fly stand-by and plan her work schedule around visiting me in Chicago. The long-distance relationship was stressful and difficult, but our bond was strong enough to get us through the rough patches. We continued to see each other as often as possible.

The end of June 1990 approached. When I completed my last year of residency training in Chicago, I had one final commitment to the military: I needed to attend the Officer Basic Course because I'd accepted the rank of lieutenant when I graduated from ROTC. The army required me to complete the three-month course at Fort Sam Houston, San Antonio, Texas. It was another stroke of luck for both Leslie and me. A short tour of duty for me turned out to be a blessing in disguise. We could see each other with relative ease; it was only a two-and-a-half-hour drive to Corpus Christi. We could plan the opening of my practice.

It truly seemed everything was taking a turn for the better and falling into place perfectly. I had been dreading taking three months out of my life to complete yet another military course, and instead it proved to be a win/win situation. I was able to save some money, plan a future, and start my practice. During that time, Leslie and I grew closer, and the inevitable M-word was drawing me deeper and deeper under its spell.

We had been dating for almost four years by now, and I felt in my heart that this was the right time to ask her to marry me. I'd purchased a ring the last time I was home in Rhode Island. I was planning for just the right moment, the perfect restaurant, flowers, and the proposal of a lifetime. That's how I envisioned the perfect proposal for us. As it turned out, the actual event was quite different from what I had anticipated.

During one of Leslie's visits to San Antonio, we had discussed marriage but never decided on anything concrete. I felt that Leslie was getting the impression I was never going to propose. Again, this was far from the case; I knew what I wanted, but I wanted to do it under my terms, like everything else. Still, with me being so close to getting on one knee and her frustration at a higher level than usual, I figured I'd forego all my careful planning in favor of putting her mind at ease. Forget the true romanticism with the restaurant, the champagne, the flowers, and the caviar; I built up my courage and decided to ask her through the bathroom door! I pushed my hand past the bathroom door and showed her the ring. It was original and definitely as romantic a setting one could get, with fluorescent lighting and the smell of Mr. Clean. It wasn't something you'd read in a romance novel, but it was very original nonetheless!

Despite the less-than-fairytale setting, she replied with an immediate, "Yes!"

I had asked Leslie to marry me at Fort Sam Houston, Texas, in August 1990. Now, after being single for thirty-eight years and with my education now officially complete, I was ready to begin a new life, with a family that was free of fear and abuse. I was ready for a future that was completely different from my childhood.

On the other hand, was it? Had I actually sat down and engaged in some heavy self-examination? Did I realize that what had probably kept me from getting married at an earlier age was the fear of becoming a mirror image of my dad? Was I destined to repeat the cycle of fear, mistrust, and abuse? Was I going to abuse my own spouse or children? Did like really breed like?

At some point over the last few months, I'd realized I was very much in love with Leslie and that my love for her far outweighed my fear of myself. After all, hadn't I already recreated myself in my own image? My life in the military was completely independent of what had gone on at home, yet it also paralleled my upbringing. It wasn't the exact opposite of my life under Dad's barbed tongue and strong iron fist because the military definitely ruled with a strong iron fist and a barbed tongue. Maybe there was some direct correlation between the military, my father, and me, which may be why I had such a successful military career.

Taking my cue from this renewed sense of independence, I made it perfectly clear to myself that I was *not* going to abuse my future wife or children. "Like breeds like" was simply never going to apply in my case. The future was a blank slate, and I intended to write my own story, not my father's version.

The marriage proposal was a success, awkward but still a success. The date was set, the plans were in effect, and time passed quickly. Everything was going as planned for the wedding. Leslie had decided on an outdoor wedding in North Dallas at a country home. Her family had really done a wonderful job of planning the wedding and reception. It could not have been more perfect. My family, on the other hand, just needed to arrive on time. (Of course, even *that* proved to be too much of a challenge.)

Most of my family, including my mother, my sister Carol, and her children, arrived a few days early to help get things ready for the big day. My dad, along with my brother-in-law, Bill, would arrive the next day after work. Well, as luck would have it, that trip proved an interesting and amusing story in itself. Bill, an intelligent, good-natured man of Irish descent, was going to bring some presents with him on the flight to Texas with my father. One of the presents, unbeknownst to him, was one of the earlier Nintendo games, which had a plastic gun in the box.

My father and Bill entered the airport, excited about going to Texas. They had a few cocktails at the airport to celebrate the upcoming celebration. They wandered over to the line of passengers for screening, and my dad passed though with no problem. As Bill passed through security, however, his package was scanned. Suddenly several security guards zoomed in on Bill like a bass on shiner. They rushed him, grabbed him by the arms, and brought him into a back room in the blink of an eye. His head was spinning, and he had no clue as to what he had done. He repeatedly asked, "What's going on, guys? What did I do?" They remained silent and whisked him away.

The security officers quickly looked over at my father but left him alone and told him that he would have to wait patiently for Bill until they were "finished with their investigation." Dad was dumbfounded and stood there scratching his head for several minutes, watching all this commotion over Bill. He walked over to a security guard and asked, "What seems to be the problem with my son-in-law?"

The security guard responded, "Sir, we saw a weapon, a gun, in the package he sent through the scanner."

"What? A gun!" exclaimed Dad. "He's not carrying a gun!"

The officer looked at my father and politely asked him to step away from the security checkpoint and go to his departure gate or they were going to interrogate him.

My father picked up his bag, began walking to his gate, and thought, *Why would Bill be carrying a gun?*

After approximately an hour of interrogation, airport security discovered that there actually was no weapon and released him. Bill hadn't known what he was carrying in the gift-wrapped package. He was just carrying a package his wife had asked him to take to Dallas.

When my father and Bill were finally reunited in the airport, they were upset about missing their scheduled flight. This was not a good way for Mr. Grumpy and his sidekick to start a three-hour journey. The result could be disastrous for me.

As most males would do, my father and Bill decided to have a few cocktails while waiting for their next flight. They complained to each other about the plastic gun like two old men on a park bench. To make matters worse, nobody else in the family knew where they were. They hadn't called anyone, as cell phones were new on the market and nobody in the family carried one. They just knew they needed to get to Dallas and that someone would be there to meet them.

While all the hubbub with my father and Bill was going on in Boston, my soon-to-be father-in-law and I patiently waited for hours at the Dallas airport. We had no information regarding the whereabouts of the lost men's departure or arrival. We just knew they'd missed their flight for some reason and were possibly having a few beers in the airport lounge and would arrive in Dallas at some point. As with any wedding, schedules needed to be met, so I hesitantly left. The scheduled events that night were to go on as planned without the two lost souls.

My father and Bill made the next flight out, and when they arrived at the Dallas-Fort Worth airport, they had no clue what hotel they were staying at or even where the wedding was to be held. That they made it to the hotel despite their intoxication is truly amazing. Eventually they arrived safe and sound at the hotel; but their drunken attitudes didn't make things any better. They had assumed that everything would go as planned and someone would be there to pick them up. Yes, that did happen. Someone was there to pick them up at the prescribed time, but they weren't there, which made the night even more stressful for the bridal couple.

After the rehearsals, I decided I needed something to drink, anticipating that Dad was going to express his concerns about the series of events that had unfolded. Sitting between my dad and my soon-to-be father-in-law in the hotel lounge, I attempted to make the polite and necessary introductions. My father's true colors began to shine through. His belligerent attitude and slurred speech stuck out rudely during the first exchange of words.

Clearly, things were not going well for the home team at this point. I had an uncanny sense that a total disaster was rapidly approaching. In addition to the airport disaster with my dad and Bill, I had not heard from my brother. Was he delayed in the airport? Was his flight cancelled? Did he have a Nintendo as well? Or had he encountered problems before he'd even left from home? What else could have gone wrong the night before the big day? Many questions were now racing across my mind. Mike had agreed to be my best man.

Well, go figure, my guess about a disaster was right. I received an unexpected phone call from Mike, who told me that he was not going to make it to the wedding. Worst of all, he couldn't or wouldn't tell me why.

There was nothing Mike and his wife had to do other than pack and get on a plane. Everything had been laid out for them: the tuxedo, the hotel room, transportation, the whole nine yards. The conversation was short and to the point. Mike just said he wasn't coming, and that was that.

Leslie and I had waited for several years for our big day. Now I was without a best man, and there wasn't much time to find another. Though it was somewhat awkward, I turned and asked my dad to step in as my best man. Maybe Dad would change his attitude if he were honored as the best man at my wedding.

Was there someone else who could fit the role better, or was this another opportunity in disguise to make peace? Maybe this was another twist of fate for the both of us. Had I realized that despite my dad's shortcomings and poor behavior that he was still the source of my flesh and blood? I thought that this invitation would make my dad proud and extremely happy.

Yes, my dad had been in his usual drunken state the night before and had pissed me off, but I wanted him to know that despite his belligerence, ill demeanor, and drinking problems, I still loved him. I knew that my dad had taught me a valuable lesson, one that I didn't even realize I was passing down. The lesson I learned was that forgiveness is good and that it was okay to forgive someone who offended you. However, I had difficulty with the part about forgetting what had happened as a child and young adult. That replayed in my mind daily.

Our wedding ceremony was breathtaking, thanks entirely to the graciousness of my wonderful in-laws. Leslie was a rare jewel, stunningly beautiful in her silky white gown and veil with a long train. A tear trickled down my face as I thought about how beautiful she looked. It was a challenge to breathe as we exchanged vows and rings on that gorgeous Saturday morning in April. I was very proud to have my wife by my side and my dad as my best man that day.

As I reflected on the bittersweet experience of bringing the two families together, I understood that weddings often bring out both the best and the worst in people. For Leslie and me, the botched travel plans and no-show of my original best man turned out to be a test of our love for each other. We had overcome the typical wedding fiascoes and shown grace under fire. Through it all, we'd treated each other with respect, love, honor, and adoration.

Chapter 10: *New Beginnings, Old Habits*

Habit is habit and not to be flung out of the window by any man, but coaxed downstairs a step at a time.

~ **Mark Twain**

The Gulf Coast weather was gorgeous, featuring a cool ocean breeze and the rustling of palm trees. The usual coastal climate temperatures were in the seventies, with a smattering of billowy white clouds in the Popsicle-blue sky. The sunlight permeated every room in the house and made it impossible to feel anything other than the peaceful warm feeling of home.

However, I was feeling more than just the pride of ownership of my new home. It was the sense of accomplishment that my hard work had enabled us to occupy this wonderful home. Several family members who had already visited considered our new home a "paradise" and said living there was like being on what amounted to a "permanent vacation."

I knew it was very different from the housing project of my hometown of Woonsocket, Rhode Island, both inside and out. Externally, our home was something to be proud of, a spacious and well-maintained addition to the neighborhood. Inside it was just as warm and appealing, both physically and emotionally. I had grown up in a dysfunctional home, and this was my escape, my refuge, and my fortress.

This was a *home*, in every sense of the word.

It had been several years since I had moved to Corpus Christi. By now, I was spoiled by such perfect days and the beauty of our scenic, coastal home.

My parents had visited several times, but this time was going to be different. I had been waiting for a perfect time for my parents to visit, and this time it seemed to be the ideal week for them to enjoy our new home.

Ever since the bittersweet inclusion of my dad as the best man at our wedding, Leslie and I had been discussing that maybe my mother and father could live with us during the colder months and return to Rhode Island for the warmer months. I knew it would be very trying on her with my dad's drinking problem and my mother's health problems, but she had the patience and personality to help make everything work out for the best.

It might bring us closer together, leveling our rocky and disturbed past, if nothing else, I thought to myself, conveniently forgetting that line about how hard it was for old habits to die.

My dad was as stubborn as I was resistant to the idea about moving there for several months, but the suggestion about short-term visits aroused my interest. He was always ready for a short trip, a road trip, especially anything less than four days. If I was ever going to have closure on my past with my father and begin an honest, mature relationship with him, it was clear that I would have to initiate a confrontation. I couldn't go on without clearing the air of the past.

My parents wanted to get away for a few days, and what could be better than flying into Corpus Christi and spending some time in the new house? Dad always had a problem with flying because of his fear of heights, something I'd inherited. If my dad behaved himself by only having a few drinks at the airport and on the plane, then the drive from the airport to the house might be a good time for me to confront him. I decided it was time to stare those old habits in the face.

They arrived early that day. After careful consideration, I decided to wait for the evening to face off with my dad. We were only moments inside the house when Dad made a mad dash for the sun by the water. The eighty-degree pool temperature was tempting, and the tropical waterfall added a relaxing touch to our backyard oasis. What made my paradise even more attractive was the multitude of tropical flowers that surrounded the patio, including red, white, and peach hibiscus. During the day, Dad would lie on his lounge chair drinking cold cans of Schlitz and gaze out over the water. Leslie and I let him sit there, content and quiet, while we made Mom feel welcome with the typical visiting-in-law rituals of showing off the house, making special lunches, and taking the occasional shopping trip into town. Dad was content just sitting there, looking out over the Gulf Coast in deep thought.

Dad seemed content with his lawn chair and bottomless cooler, so Leslie, Mom, and I were more than happy to leave him alone. He apparently enjoyed our new home, and I commented, "Not bad for a kid coming out of the housing projects!" He responded with the same in a tone of satisfaction.

The ocean breeze and sunshine were a wonderful combination for my father. Cold weather was not his favorite, although he had absolutely no intention of leaving Rhode Island anytime soon.

His constant presence in the backyard reminded me how much he liked sitting on his own back deck in the summer. He enjoyed some simple pleasures in life, such as listening to the cardinals sing, a good ballgame, a cold beer, a comfortable rocking chair, and, preferably, as few distractions as possible. There was nothing more enjoyable to my dad than sitting on a lounge chair on a back deck or having a few beers with his friends at the club.

Many times, I looked through the window from inside the house and watched my dad just sitting there. He seemed a cold and distant figure, as always, but a compelling one nonetheless. Our history might have been complicated by violence and anger, but I still held out hope for the future.

Did I really?

My father was hard to read; he always had been. He would look out at the ocean, admiring the birds and the seascape, while I wondered what he was really thinking. What, if anything, was going through my dad's mind? Did he simply want another beer, or was he wondering where we were going to have dinner? Alternatively, was he thinking about how proud he was of his son? Did I meet his expectations after my unsuccessful attempt at professional football?

I still wonder to this day what he was thinking.

It was inevitable that I was going to let him know exactly what I was thinking, and that was about to unexpectedly happen for Dad.

As the sun slowly set on the horizon one evening, I needed to quickly intervene before my father switched from his daylong beer fest to a few of his nightly martinis. On many occasions, I could actually watch the metamorphosis happen as he switched drinks. The onset of redness in his eyes, the slurring of his speech, and the arrogant attitude were the usual signs, which I'd witnessed for many years.

Later that evening, we chose to go out and have dinner at a local restaurant with a calming and tranquil ocean view. I wanted to impress my parents again by showing them the best that Corpus Christi had to offer, and since my dad was such a fan of an ocean view, the restaurant seemed to be a perfect fit.

For her part, Mom tried her best to be the bridge among Leslie, Dad, and me. She worked hard to keep Dad engaged in the conversation as his martinis flowed, and I inconspicuously looked at her, amazed that she'd tolerated this behavior for so many years. It was clear how long she'd been compensating for the old man's weaknesses. Years and years of playing the straight man to his wild and wooly ways; apologizing endlessly for his callous comments and quick temper; remaining on the outskirts of polite society thanks to his bad temper and worse manners—she'd done it all.

How much had marrying my father cost her emotionally, physically, and psychologically over the years?

I shook off the negative vibes and set out to enjoy the evening. But in the back of my mind, I was destined for the confrontation. Much had happened over the past few years, and look where I'd landed. I had a blossoming new career, a beautiful wife, and a warm, inviting home, and now my parents were here to enjoy my hard-earned life.

It was turning out to be a wonderful family night, and everything was just perfect: the food, the music, and the reflection of the stars and moon dancing off the water like diamonds on black velvet. My mother was sitting right next to me, enjoying her seafood dinner. She was clueless about the mission I was preparing to embark on. My mother was about to get an earful, and we were about to relive the fear we'd once encountered from Dad's ability to change personalities thanks to alcohol.

I felt terrible that my mother was about to experience something like this, but there was no doubt about it, it had to be done. I wasn't doing this just for me, but for her as well. The entire family was linked by our shared past of violence, fear, and intimidation. We had all experienced different forms of brutality and abuse from my father. I couldn't hold my head high and live as a self-respecting man without facing the demons of my past. I was about to take the devil by the horns and look him right in the eyes.

Many mothers have the psychic ability to sense things before they happen to a family member, especially their children, and she possibly sensed the tension in the air. Could Leslie also have sensed that something like this could happen? Was that why she kept pushing me for my parents to visit? I was physically ready for the encounter with Dad, but was I emotionally ready? Was my father ready? Did it matter? I could question myself all night long, but the time loomed near. Ready or not, I prepared myself to take the leap. I knew that the pleasant evening would soon turn into a devastating martini night, but I was eager to find salvation; however, this brought little more satisfaction than kicking a sleeping dog. I dropped the gloves, and now was the time to confront him about his cruel and abusive behavior.

As my father took another sip from his martini, I looked him directly in the eye. Without blinking, I said, "Dad, why were you so mean and abusive to us when we were younger?"

He calmly finished his sip of martini, placed the glass on the table, and appeared barely shocked. He didn't seem to understand why I was asking him such a question or to even understand the subject matter. His selective memory, of course, had no recollection of cruelty or abusiveness. Or maybe he just wanted to enjoy the evening and avoid the subject entirely.

In fact, quite the opposite was true; he thought he'd been a *good* father.

He quickly and gruffly replied, "What are you talking about?"

Using a firm and direct voice, which he wasn't accustomed to hearing from one of his own children, I said, "Dad, you used to beat us almost every Friday and Saturday night when you came home from the club!"

Raising his voice and sticking his chest out, he said, "I did not!"

Prepared not to back down, I again looked him in the eye and said, "Dad, you beat us nearly every Friday and Saturday night when you came home from the club! Please don't deny it. One of the things you forbade me to do was lie, so please don't lie to me!"

I proceeded to explain in detail how he would viciously beat all of us, except our sister, and how Michael received the brunt of the physical and emotional abuse. "Dad," I continued, "I watched you throw Michael across the room into the reclining chair, and I received a severe beating with a pepper shaker because I didn't know the difference between an umpire and a referee! You would also beat Mom and call her terrible names whenever you felt like it. I watched you beat her in the bathtub until she was almost unconscious one night!

"Why? Why did you do that to us? We never tried to hurt you. Please don't tell me you don't remember! I won't accept that!"

There was total silence at the table. I could see my father's eyes beginning to water as he said with a trembling voice, "I thought I was a good father. I don't remember doing anything like that!"

I was hitting a nerve, and he didn't like it; but I was finally accomplishing my mission, and he began to understand. I knew my dad needed to realize what he had done before it was too late; his abusive behavior was not going to be left swept under the carpet. He was going to know before his wife passed away or before any of us wanted to let bygones be bygones that he'd been downright abusive.

I had to clear the air, not just for my own benefit but also for the entire family.

Responding calmly, I said, "Dad, you, in your own way, and Mom *were* good parents. Think about how we all turned out. We all have good jobs; we've never been to prison." However, I kept that one night I spent in jail for beating two men in the back of my mind. "Your children turned out well, and you're lucky Mom stayed with you. You were just abusive, and we never knew why. Can't you help us understand so we can move on with our lives? So you and Mom can too?"

Tears rolled down his face and Mom's as well. The granite look of fear I'd expected, that deer-caught-in-the-headlights look, was nowhere to be found. Dad was completely surprised. So was Mom, although she seemed content and at peace with the confrontation, knowing that otherwise it never would have happened. I was confident that she never would have done it herself. It would have stayed under the carpet for our entire lives.

Mom either loved my father so much that she didn't want to upset the apple cart or was so afraid of triggering another violent reaction that she'd never discuss the matter on her own. Maybe she wanted to forget it ever happened. I couldn't do that. In fact, I was ashamed for letting it go so long. To this day, I still question my manliness for not acting sooner, recalling the day I jumped on his back.

I flashed back to a previous life, one in which violence was an almost daily routine and one I thought I could outgrow merely by becoming a man and starting a family. The memory came rushing back …

***

In fifth grade, I sat in the front row; I was somewhat of a mischievous child, and the teacher wanted to keep a close eye on my behavior. This was back when kids had plastic peashooters; a few of us would put in a few cents to purchase a box of peas. We had daily wars with peashooters. It just so happened that one day I found a pea on the classroom floor. I picked it up and began to play with it as I sat at my desk waiting for the bell to ring and release us for the day.

It was just my luck that as I was playing with the pea, I flipped it too hard, and it bounced right across the teacher's desk. I guess the teacher was having a bad day as well; she was probably as eager as the rest of us were for the final bell to ring. Now, just moments before the end of the day, I'd gone and made a bad day worse.

She looked at me with an evil eye and told me to stand up. Of course, I was an obedient child, despite being a mischievous ten-year-old boy. As I rose to my feet, I watched her reach into her desk drawer and pull out the infamous eighteen-inch wooden ruler she used to discipline the unlucky or unruly souls. It had no name, but it was the fear of the classroom nonetheless.

I wasn't the only one to see the ruler come out of her drawer. The room became extremely quiet, and I knew exactly what to expect. Corporal punishment was still widely accepted in the early 1960s, and, like many of her peers, my teacher was not afraid to use it. As she marched over to my desk, she glared at me and said, "Why did you shoot that at me?"

I replied in a defensive yet fearful voice, "Mrs. Dwyer, I didn't shoot that at you on purpose. It was an accident."

She growled, "Put your hands out in front of you with palms up, now!"

I slowly pulled my hands from behind my back and placed my palms up in front of my body. I was hoping she was just bluffing and trying to scare me. I was hoping she was waiting until the bell rang so she could save face in front of the students. I was wrong, and I knew it the minute I felt the stinging pain and heard the sound of the crack as she struck my left hand with the ruler. She wound up with that ruler as if she were John Wayne getting ready to throw a haymaker—a type of punch that a man would throw in a street fight, powerful enough to knock out the other man.

The pain was excruciating, but I wasn't going to cry no matter how badly it hurt. Instinctively, I went into defense mode and grabbed her right wrist, the one attached to the hand holding the ruler. I then cocked my right fist and said, "Don't you touch me again!"

This was no shrinking violet or substitute teacher. Mrs. Dwyer was as old-school as they come; she knew how to get, and keep, the upper hand. Without blinking, she gritted her teeth. I knew I was done for when she said, "Let me go, or I'll call your father!"

I knew that if I didn't let her go, the pain I'd receive later that night from my father would be ten times more severe. So I let her go and immediately put both hands back out in front of me so she could continue administering my undeserved punishment for an honest mistake.

I would much rather have her beat me than go home and face the wrath of my father, especially while he was under the influence of alcohol and embarrassed about receiving a call from my teacher.

Despite the beating, I had to give old Mrs. Dwyer credit; at least she kept the incident secret from my Dad.

***

Back at the restaurant, the memory flashed through my mind as I watched Dad wrestle with his own emotions. No doubt, the evening was a painful and a revelatory one for him, and I'm sure he wished I'd kept the secret as well. Nevertheless, unlike Mrs. Dwyer, I knew that burying the past was no way to deal with it. Only by uncovering the skeletons, dusting them off, and bringing them into the light could we hope to rid ourselves of the past once and for all.

That fateful dinner might not have had a nice, neat, four-hankie Hollywood ending, but I'd done what I'd set out to do. Confronting my father wasn't about self-satisfaction; it was more about self-respect. I knew this conversation wouldn't change my father's ways. He wasn't about to go to rehab because he didn't think he had a drinking problem; but he knew he was abusive and chose to ignore that problem. The ultimate goal that night was to make sure he knew the truth about his abusive behavior and hope that he would get professional help. That would never happen.

I looked forward to new beginnings and put the past to rest.

Chapter 11: *The Final Salute*

When a man blames others for his failures, it's a good idea to credit others with his successes.

~ Howard W. Newton

Mosul, Iraq, June 2005. It was business as usual in the Tactical Operations Center (TOC), just another hectic day battling the global war on terrorism, complete with radios crackling, telephones ringing, conversations blaring, and a dozen spitting keyboards tapping. If it weren't for the guerrilla warfare and daily violence that raged just outside the sandbagged front door, you could imagine that the noises were coming from a comforting office building in suburban America.

Outside the sandbag-covered entryway of TOC, the sounds became more sinister with every step you took. Merely by poking your head out the door, you could hear random insurgent attacks with incoming mortars and rockets, complete with the popping of small-arms fire and the whizzing of an occasional stray round.

Meanwhile, the afternoon call to prayer bellowing from the local mosques had just begun to echo throughout the city. The sound of helicopters and C-130s drowned out the locals' eerie wailing of "Allah Akbar."

Life was becoming a twenty-four-hour battle that was only partially being fought in this godforsaken desert. It didn't matter where the desert was. It didn't have to be in Iraq; it could have been a desert in the United States. Whatever the case, the desert was hot, dry, and downright miserable. Focusing on my daily duties in the TOC was difficult; I was overwhelmed with the ever-present possibility of a direct rocket attack, caring for the wounded, thinking about my father's worsening condition, and remembering my life back home.

It was battle fatigue in every sense of the word; only this war had been raging since I was a boy. Despite growing older and even confronting my dad, I had yet to see a flag of surrender.

Until now.

News from home was bad, and it was going to get worse before it got better. I'd had several conversations via satellite phone or e-mail with Carol in recent weeks, all of which made me realize that my dad's health was declining rapidly. Daily, I anticipated an emergency message from the Red Cross regarding my father's poor health, fearing that he wasn't expected to make it through the week. Indeed, the notification from my sister finally did flash across my desk, recommending that I depart Iraq for Rhode Island as soon as possible.

An ugly sensation vibrated deep within my bones; the inevitable was near.

Most military personnel would leap at the chance to escape the rigors of the political and personal pressure that encompassed the conflict in Iraq, but not me. At least in the desert there was a chance for survival. Where I was headed, death seemed certain and, quite possibly, sudden.

Packing only the necessary personal items, I started the long, twenty-two-hour trek back to the United States for a bittersweet homecoming. There was no need for thick bestsellers or in-flight magazines to keep my mind occupied. Long-buried skeletons and new concerns kept my mind captive for the full-day flight.

How could it be so wonderful to see my family under such dire circumstances, even after so many months in Iraq? Could I feel both joy and sadness? I knew from my sister how quickly and irrevocably Dad's health had declined. How could such a strong and powerful man, who had once ruled with an iron fist, now be so weak, frail, and humble?

Of course, the old man wasn't so weak that he couldn't still make life interesting for those who loved and feared him. Specifically, my dad made a special request that I visit him in the hospital wearing my desert camouflage uniform (DCU). Although he didn't talk about it much, he must have always been secretly proud of my accomplishments and my service in the Army Reserves. It pleased him even more when I was promoted to lieutenant colonel and deployed to serve our country in Iraq. In addition, although he would never admit to it when we were growing up, I suspected that my father had *always* been proud of his children. But should we make excuses for our parents' ill behavior? Do we turn our heads in denial and say that the terrible things they did aren't really representative of who they are?

Dad never knew how to show it, let alone how to say it. I used to watch my friends with their fathers as we grew up. They were big, strong men too, but not so big and strong that they were afraid to show affection for their own kids. My dad was different. He was a disciplinarian who demanded respect, and that's exactly what he got from his children and his wife. But it was respect out of fear and intimidation, not adoration. As I thought about the DCU in my duffle bag, I thought about how little things had changed.

All three of his children knew how to listen and obey his unspoken command just from his look. It was the *look*, that specific look, the look that says a thousand words, and you understand every word of it. If you ignored that look, you could expect to suffer the consequences.

Every parent has "the look," but while most parents follow it up with a time-out or a reduction in allowance, we always knew that our father's look implied that the threat was real, swift, and absolute violence.

The long, lonely flight home offered me plenty of time to think and reminisce about the past, present, and future. I thought about the soldiers, civilians, and children who had died before my eyes over the past eight months. The lives of some very young men and women had been cut short or changed forever simply because they stood up for their beliefs with the selfless intention of wanting to make a better life for themselves, those back home, and even total strangers.

Those in the military know the ultimate sacrifice that hovers over us all, but we voluntarily raised our hands with free will and in good faith, swearing to stand behind the commander in chief's decisions.

I thought about the long-term impact of the violence and wondered what many of the kids on the operating room table had experienced back home before coming to Iraq. Had they been prepared for the violence of warfare? The swift and brutal whims of fate brought death in the guise of mortar shells, car bombs, or early morning ambushes.

The threat of violence in Iraq was constantly palpable and exhausting, and I was constantly reminded of home. It was a trigger of the fear I felt walking home every day after school, or waiting for my dad to come home every night.

The difference was that the violence in the desert was swift and sudden, coming in the form of violent strangers doing violent things. At home, we fought a silent battle, and the pain was more personal than physical. Every punch was a betrayal of the bond between father and son; every tear shed was a wasted opportunity for love and respect.

I knew that the physical and emotional scars of many of the patients would last for years and that the healing process had barely begun. Selfishly, I wondered how long I would have to grieve for my own lost childhood and whether or not this last visit to see my dad would finally bring some closure.

Finally, the aircraft pulled up to the gate at the Providence airport. Walking past security, I was greeted with tears by Carol. Her grief was clear, her face lined with pain and worry. It made me realize that the battle she had been fighting on the home front was an arduous and losing one as well.

We briefly exchanged hugs and tears. Carol could say only a few words: "I love you, and I'm glad you're home!" I made an effort to remain outwardly strong and confident, but inside I was falling apart with grief.

We gathered up my bags, loaded the car, and made the short trip north to the quaint hospital in Woonsocket, Rhode Island. On the way, Carol broke the surprising news that our mom had also been admitted to the hospital and was in the same ward and on the same floor as our dad. Mom's condition was not as serious as Dad's was, but it nonetheless required our attention. What a greeting: both parents in the hospital. I was barely awake from jet lag and had only minutes to digest and assess the situation.

Could the home front be as dangerous as the battlefield I'd left behind?

We silently walked from the hospital parking lot into the main lobby and rode the elevator to the fourth floor. Carol tried to prepare me for the worst, but her words of concern and compassion were ignored. I was sleepwalking between the past and the present, equal parts grown man approaching his dying father and scared little boy awaiting yet another beating.

Walking into my dad's room, I noticed his thin, drawn, and pale condition; he exhibited all the signs of a seriously sick person. It took all the control I had not to show my shock at how badly he'd deteriorated since the last time we saw each other. I made every attempt not to be obvious about the fact that he didn't look very well at all.

As I leaned over, kissed him on his forehead, and said a worried hello, the first words out of his mouth were, "Show me your lieutenant colonel rank!" He gave me a quick head to toe inspection and said, "Son, I am proud of you!"

At last, he was a proud father, and he was in all his glory that awesome day. Dad displayed that fulfilled expression of a happy parent, so rarely seen in the past and yet so genuine now. It was one of the few moments I could remember where my father was content with me. I was a field grade officer in the United States Army and serving in combat in Iraq for Operation Iraqi Freedom—all while bearing his own last name.

The visit was sweet but subdued. After his initial burst of patriotism and pride, my dad slowly faded. He just didn't have the physical strength to rally for too long. Dad kept nodding in and out of sleep, so Carol and I wandered down the hall to see our mom.

As we walked into her room, Mom looked pale and wan, but in a far better state than my father; she had her usual big smile on her face. We exchanged warm greetings and visited her as long as the hospital would allow. The nursing staff treated us with tremendous respect and made gracious exceptions for us, considering I'd just arrived from Iraq.

Carol and I continued the visit as long as possible until they both began to fade for the evening. I said my good-byes to my parents with a heavy heart and tore myself away from their bedsides. I promised that I would return every day that they were in the hospital.

We needed to leave the hospital, as it was way after visiting hours. Driving back to Carol's home, I barely could stay awake. After I walked into Carol's home and greeted her family, it didn't take long for me to ask for a bed. My journey had been long and exhausting from battling the demons in my head; otherwise, I surely would have tossed and turned until sunrise.

I visited my parents daily, as I'd promised; Mom recovered and was released only a day or two after I returned home. Although she was somewhat fatigued and weak, she demanded to accompany me to visit Dad, and together we continued to make the daily visits to see him in the hospital. Mom was doing fine, but Dad seemed to worsen over the next few days. I will never forget the look on my dad's face on one specific day. It was the look of fear, innocence, and insecurity, like a child without a home.

He'd been waiting for days to go home, and his doctor did not feel he was ready to leave the hospital. Dad was anxious and at the same time childlike, at the mercy of his physician and mentally crossing his fingers, hoping things would go his way. It was obvious that the roles between father and son were now reversed. Thanks to the cruel and unforgiving hands of time, my dad appeared to be a child again. He looked like a boy who had just been told the World Series had been rained out and his front-row tickets would be going to waste.

Before long he was crying and said, "I want to go home! John, I want to go home!"

I steeled myself against my own emotions, unprepared for the sudden role reversal. Finally, I replied in a tone of understanding and concern, "Dad, you're not strong enough to take care of yourself yet. You have to prove to me that you're capable of taking care of yourself first. Mom is just not physically strong enough to help you at home right now, and I have to leave in a few short days."

He looked at me with his once-powerful look of domination and determination and said, "Not strong enough? I'll show you who's not strong enough!" He struggled to stand and said, "Help me get up; I'm going to walk around this floor! I just want to go home."

I helped my dad to his feet; he was that determined to go home. I watched this now-frail old man as he wobbled to stand, heartbroken to see a physically powerful man become so weak and dependent before my eyes. I thought that this man couldn't be my father; he was someone else now.

Over the next week, Dad did whatever he could to strengthen himself so he could finally prove to his doctors that he was strong enough to go home. They finally released him. I was able to help him at home over the next few days and observed that my mother would have some difficulty assisting him. Carol would do as much as she could to help, but I knew in my heart that it would be difficult for me to leave when the time came.

As the end of my emergency leave approached, I cherished this precious time with my father and mother. The day quickly came when I had to return to duty. Leaving my parents and returning to Iraq was a day I'll never forget. I'd been home for nearly two weeks, helping my dad recover and doing things for my mom around the house. She was tired and scared of the prospect of facing the challenge alone, but she continued to endure with all her might. You could see the concern in her eyes as she worried about the fate of her husband, her son, and her own uncertain future.

I marveled at the irony. She'd endured untold abuse at the hands of her husband, yet she was now his sole caregiver. Amazingly, she faced her new role as the provider with the same stoic heroism with which she'd faced those endless years of abuse. Perhaps it was duty that propelled her out of bed in the morning to tend to her husband all day, but she couldn't hide the look of love and devotion that flashed across her face from time to time.

Talk about unconditional love. I thought of how closely it paralleled the sacrifices made by those in the military. Her wedding vows were her enlistment papers, and her own personal war was never-ending. Now she faced the final battle alone, a fierce warrior despite her calm, graceful demeanor. I was astonished at her courage as she sadly watched me organize my belongings before leaving for the airport.

It was a somber morning and mostly quiet around the house; the ticking cuckoo clock filled the house like an eight-hundred-pound gorilla. Mom was limping with pain from her severe arthritis and the several knee surgeries she'd recently endured. She was a very tough and stubborn woman.

Sitting outside on the red-stained deck, Dad was enjoying the beautiful New England summer weather, as he'd done for many years, while teetering in the same worn-out, weathered rocking chair. I was inside the house and began packing my bags, preparing to leave for my two o'clock flight back to Iraq. I wondered what thoughts were going through my dad's mind. Was he contemplating more than just the familiar quiet of the street and backyard?

Was he simply enjoying the scenery, which included red maples, blue spruce pines, and oak trees, and listening to the songs of the cardinals as they flew from tree to tree? Maybe he was focused on the warm, gentle summer breeze and the heat of the sun on his face. Was he reflecting on his life? Was he thinking of the manner in which he'd raised his children and wondering if he'd been a good father? As usual, I couldn't tell, and time was running out fast. I knew this might be the last time I'd see my father alive.

Wanting to have a few words with him just in case it was indeed the last time, I walked out the back door onto the deck and gave him a smile. His chair eerily creaked as he slowly rocked back and forth. That sight caused me to pause and take a deep breath as I tried to maintain my composure. The cowboy hat he wore was a gift from me, purchased during his initial visit to Corpus Christi. Did he wear that hat to display a hidden message of warmth, respect, and gratitude, or was it just the closest covering available?

Although he appeared frail and weak with pallid skin and significant weight loss, he seemed somewhat comfortable and unafraid. He looked up at me with a simple smile on his face and didn't appear to be in any pain. I sat in the chair next to him, and the deep breath I'd taken earlier proved useless; I began to cry. The little boy of many years past was now crying for a different reason. The tears flooded my eyes as I repeatedly told him that I loved him while I kissed his hand, kissed his hand, and kissed his hand.

I said with a cracking voice, "I wanted you to be proud of me."

He replied with a broken smile, "I always have been. I need you to be strong as I always have been, because you are the new leader of this family."

The parting of ways was proving extremely difficult for both of us, although we knew it was something that had to be done since it was time for me to return to Iraq. As we said our final good-byes and exchanged a warm embrace, he said "so long" as he always had; he never wanted to say good-bye. Saying good-bye was too final for him. I didn't want to let him go.

I sobbed, "Dad, don't you go and die on me. You have to wait until I come home because if you do I'll never talk to you again."

With a grin, he replied sarcastically, "If I do, you'll kill me, won't you?"

We both laughed a little bit and then I gave him the hug I'd so desired as a child. I lifted his hat off his head and kissed him on his forehead. I couldn't turn around and look back at my father as I walked into the house. I happened to notice that on my way back inside that my sister had overheard our conversation. She was sitting at the same kitchen table that had been the center of many years of violence and was crying as well.

A few moments later, Dad slowly shuffled back into the house and headed directly into his bedroom without saying a word. We heard the sound of someone rattling through a dresser drawer, searching for something.

It was only a matter of minutes before he emerged from his room, walked over to me, and said with a quivering voice, "I want you to have this." Digging into his shirt pocket, he pulled out a handsome ruby and gold ring. He reached for my right hand and placed it in the center of my palm, wrapped his hands around my fingers, and said, "This was my father's ring. It's very precious to me, and I want you to have it. It's important to me that you have this ring."

I stood silently for a moment and then calmly looked into my father's eyes. I said "Dad, now this ring has become very important to me! I'll treasure it always." I hugged and kissed him one last time. He never explained why he wanted me to have the ring, but the implication was obvious. He turned, walked back outside, and sat in his favorite chair.

Turning to my wife, I put the irreplaceable heirloom in the palm of her hand. I didn't intend to bring the ring back with me to Iraq for obvious reasons, and I asked her to keep it in a safe place until my return. I never saw my grandfather's ruby ring again.

Gathering my bags and looking at my wife, I said, "That was the most difficult thing I've ever done." My dad was telling me good-bye in his own way and wanted me to have something to remember him by. I made a valiant attempt to hold myself together and catch my breath, but my eyes overflowed with tears. I shouldered my bags and walked down the stairs toward the front door.

Carol planned to drive me back to the airport that afternoon. I knew she was looking forward to the day when I finally returned from Iraq as much as our mother was. Despite her sadness to see her brother depart, however, she had to resume the huge, time-consuming, and emotionally draining responsibility of taking care of our ill parents alone.

Walking out the front door of my parents' home to load my luggage into the car, I felt someone watching me. I looked over my right shoulder and noticed my dad standing on the back deck, wearing his cowboy hat. Our eyes met, and at that instant, he snapped to attention and gave me a sharp salute. The salute was crisp and strong as though given by a man twenty years his junior. I quickly dropped my bags where I stood and proudly came to attention, returning the honor, respect, and professional courtesy.

The hair on the back of my neck and arms stood at attention. My heart began pounding inside my chest. Our hearts had finally connected. I knew subconsciously that this exchange was going to be our last on earth.

During that brief moment, my dad displayed the ultimate sign of respect and delivered a message to me, asking for more than forgiveness. I never said a word because his eyes had clearly portrayed his remorseful sincerity. As a chill raced throughout my body and pierced my heart, I knew we were never going to see each other alive on this planet again. The inevitable was near.

Throughout my military career, I'd rendered many salutes with respect and courtesy to countless high-ranking officers and distinguished officials. There remains no doubt that the most important and memorable exchange of salutes in my life is the salute I rendered to my dad that fateful day. It truly was an unforgettable salute.

We loaded what little possessions I had into the car. Amazingly enough, as we pulled out of the driveway, Dad was bending over the porch railing, waving a final good-bye. I turned to my wife, grasped her hand, and said, "This is the toughest day of my life, and I'll never forget it. Thank you for being here with me."

That was the last time I spoke with my dad and the last time I saw him alive.

The drive to the airport was quick, and we spoke few words in the car. Even as we entered the terminal and I checked in with the ticket agent, we were silent. I mentioned to the agent that I was returning to Iraq. She suggested under the circumstances that she would allow my family to visit with me at the gate until departure.

We were extremely grateful that the agent had permitted us another hour together before I left. The time passed quickly, and the call came for all passengers to board the aircraft. I gave my usual bear hugs and told everyone not to worry about me because I was a good soldier and, most of all, just plain lucky. I told them I loved them, asked them to look after Dad, and walked away.

Thinking back to my dad's last request, I presented myself as very manly and displayed a façade of strength. As I walked to the gate and began to walk down the jet-bridge, I turned one more time, smiled, and gave a last good-bye before my long, lonely journey back to Iraq.

Chapter 12: *Burying the Past*

A little more than two months after returning to Iraq, I received a second communication from the Red Cross. This morbid message was that my father had passed away. My dad had finally succumbed to his struggle with a disease of the heart called cardiac amyloidosis. I packed my bags again for another twenty-four-hour journey back to Rhode Island. It was a serious reason to return home, but it was the more dangerous method of leaving and reentering a combat zone that made me nervous.

I dreaded the combat landings and take-offs of the C-130 aircraft. They were a necessary evil and a tactic employed to avoid antiaircraft fire. The G-forces produced were so tremendous from the twisting, turning, and rapidly changing altitude of the aircraft that I actually felt my combat helmet lift off my head. This maneuver made me violently ill. I had the dry heaves so badly that the blood vessels in my face burst.

Thanks to the hard work and experience of our operations and human resource officers, the tedious, complex process of getting me back home went rather smoothly. The coordination required to return any soldier to the United States was an amazing feat in itself. Despite their intensive efforts just to get me out of Iraq in a timely manner, there were still the layovers in Kuwait and Germany, which could greatly impede my travels. Factoring in the current combat situation, bad weather, and any shamals, a form of desert sandstorm in Persia, it was possible I could be delayed several days and miss the funeral altogether.

There was a narrow window of opportunity to exit Iraq, and I was cutting it very close, with only three days to get to Rhode Island. On the brighter side, the twenty-four-hour time difference between Iraq and the United States gave me a day to spare. Getting home was paramount, but, once again, the gut-wrenching liftoff and bumpy air travel were far from my favorite things to do.

It was extremely hot that day, and a mirage was glaring off the runway. The C-130 taxied up to the passenger load ramp with all four engines running in what sounded like perfect synchronization. The noxious fumes of the exhaust mixed with the smell of jet fuel, making my already-nervous stomach even queasier. We were only minutes away from takeoff, and my anxiety level intensified as I eagerly entered through the rear of the aircraft. I inched my way forward to the front and sat on a red nylon mesh seat. The seats were lightweight, stored easily, and designed for paratroopers with large combat loads, not for comfort. I buckled my seat belt and mentally prepared myself for the inevitable ride from hell.

The whining of the tailgate lifting and slamming closed was the signal that we'd soon be on our way. All doors were securely fastened. The aircraft taxied to the beginning of the runway and paused; up to this point, everything seemed normal. We waited for a short while and then patiently waited a little longer, but now it was nearly an hour later and we still were waiting to take off. The weather conditions appeared to be good for flying, but maybe there was a mechanical problem or combat situation causing the delay. The temperature in Iraq that day was over 125 degrees; on the tarmac, it was definitely higher. Inside the aircraft, it felt like a dry sauna that burned when you breathed in deeply. The air-conditioning was off, probably to conserve fuel. The temperature was rising, and a full load of combat equipment made the situation worse. It was nearly intolerable and brutally miserable, but I just wanted to be airborne.

Like a breath of fresh air, the engines roared, and the aircraft began picking up speed and moved down the runway. We were soon airborne and on our way to Kuwait. I tolerated the temporary nausea and vomiting from the liftoff, knowing I was traveling in the right direction.

Suddenly, the aircraft slowed in mid-air, which was different from the usual takeoffs. We were already about twenty minutes into the flight when I felt the aircraft make a 180-degree turn and begin to make a combat descent.

We landed safely on the airfield, all soldiers deplaned immediately, and we waited in the terminal for news regarding our flight. Later, I found out that one of the four engines had failed, and the pilot had made a wise decision to make an emergency landing.

We waited on the ground for a few more hours until air operations replaced the aircraft. We proceeded once again with the usual boarding, and I anticipated the stomach-turning takeoff once more. I hadn't looked into a mirror, but I assumed my face looked like a road map with all the broken blood vessels from the dry heaves. The only consolation to this flight was that I knew there was going to be a normal landing in Kuwait, and the next flight out of Kuwait was going to be on a commercial aircraft like a Boeing 737.

As we arrived in Kuwait, the atmosphere changed and the stress of combat began to lessen. I'd been in Kuwait no more than a day when our aircraft was ready to return to the United States with a stop in Germany to refuel. I was on my way home.

During the long journey, I faded in and out of my surroundings, facing my father's demons, which continuously haunted me. I struggled to make peace with them and my father. It was like being trapped in time. I knew my family was already together, grieving in unison as I grieved alone, and I was unable to share their pain. Was I always destined to be a day late and a dollar short even for my father's funeral, and maybe even my own? Was history about to repeat itself for me?

After more than a full day of travel, the aircraft landed in the United States and pulled into the gate. The seat belt sign clicked off, and I was slapped in the face by reality. Exiting through the door of the aircraft, I looked down the jet-bridge; it seemed like a vanishing point, a never-ending tunnel to what awaited me.

Emerging from the jet-bridge, I regained consciousness and passed through security into the tearful embrace of my sister. She wore a smile of mixed emotions. We hugged as if tomorrow was our last day on earth and cried for several minutes.

Between gasps for breath, we said how much we loved each other as we stood in the middle of the airport. We were reliving a scene that had happened nearly two months ago; but this time there was closure. We barely said another word, and an uncomfortable silence settled over us. I leaned over and picked up my bags, looked up at Carol, and gave her a smile of reassurance. I wrapped my arm around her shoulders, and we walked to her car.

During the drive home, our conversation was brief, focusing on my mother's state of health and the question of what lay ahead for her.

"Carol, how is Mom doing? Is she okay?" I asked softly.

"She's okay, but she's in a state of disbelief," Carol replied.

We pulled up to Mom's matchbox-sized home, which had green siding, white shutters, and a wooden rail fence. I shrugged off some serious jet lag, breathed deeply, walked into the house, and greeted my mother with a bear hug. This hug was better than any embrace I'd given her in the past. Tears were streaming down our faces as we were finally able to reconnect. She was happy to see me, even if it was under the worst conditions.

We gathered around the kitchen table and discussed the events of the next few days. We talked about the wake, the church service, and the cemetery services, but Mom and Dad were one step ahead of us. If there was anything my father and mother had prepared for, it was the untimely nature of their deaths. They had prepaid for their gravesites, the funeral, and the church services. Their headstones, caskets, and the veterans' service for Dad were already lined up. They'd made their own decisions, and there was little to discuss as far as services went.

The conversation soon shifted, and a silence filled the room. I asked Carol to tell me about Dad's last few moments on earth, and she began the story. She set the stage, telling me that he'd had some difficulty breathing and was barely conscious but appeared to be in very little pain. She continued to explain that Dad tried to hang in there until I completed my tour of duty and safely returned from Iraq. She knew he wanted to keep his promise, the one he'd made to me during our last conversation on the back deck.

Under the heavy weight of grief, Carol took us back one week in time, describing her final tearful minutes with Dad. She was at home a week ago Wednesday morning when she received a telephone call from the hospice nurse at the rehab center. She explained how Dad's physician recommended that Dad should be cared for at this facility because Mom was unable to assist him.

The floor nurse suggested that Carol should have Mom and any other family members come to the hospice as soon as possible. She further explained that his vital signs were deteriorating and that his time was rapidly approaching.

It was in her opinion, and that of the doctor, that my Dad's instability might not allow him to survive through the day. Carol immediately begged them to let her take him home so he could die in his own bed, in his own home, where he belonged. His time was short, however, and the medical professionals feared that he might pass away en route, in an ambulance instead of in his own bed.

Carol, with full composure, quickly made the necessary calls to get all the close family members to the hospice immediately because it wasn't going to be much longer. The morphine flowing through his veins eased his pain and slurred his speech. He struggled to mumble a few last words. Carol thought he was asking for water, but as she listened more closely, what he was really saying was that he loved us. Carol held back her tears.

Mom sat by his side and sang to him their honeymoon song, "Honey," which they both dearly loved. Her singing slowly brought back his crooked smile. Carol held his hand and placed cool compresses on his forehead while waiting for the inevitable final chapter in his life to come to a close.

The nurse walked into the room, and Dad was very restless, twitching his legs and jerking his body. Carol asked, "Why is he so restless?" The nurse looked at her and said, "It's possible that he has some unresolved issues that are bothering him." Carol gave it some thought and recalled the promise that he'd made to me that day on the back deck.

She waited for the room to be quiet. Mom was fatigued and needed to lie down on the empty bed next to Dad and rest. She was showing signs of mental and physical exhaustion from the stress she'd endured over the last few weeks.

Dad was growing weaker and weaker, and Carol realized his time was near. She gently stroked his hand, and tears trickled down her face. Taking a deep breath and gathering her courage, she leaned over and gently whispered into his ear, "Dad, I know you're trying to keep your promise to John and hang on until he gets home, but if you can't, it's okay. John won't be mad at you, and he'll understand. If you want to go, it's okay. John will understand and not hold you to your promise. He'll still love you, and he knows you love him too."

As he continued his shallow breaths, he closed his eyes and never opened them again. Carol whispered in his ear, "Your father and your brother are waiting for you. Although we'll miss you, your dad and Uncle Eddie miss you even more. They'll be happy to see you again." He wearily brought back his crooked smile.

Carol put the Red Sox game on the television so he could hear it, and she described the plays. All the time she held his hand so he'd know that when it was time to go he wasn't alone. He never said another word. With a subtle smile on his face, he took his last breath and peacefully passed away.

I was proud of my sister and her family for having the courage to be there when our dad and mom needed someone the most. I will always bear the guilt that I missed the once-in-a-lifetime opportunity to say my respectful good-byes and truly make peace with my father.

Over the next few days, we discussed who would deliver the eulogy at the church. I asked everyone if I could read the short story I wrote regarding my visit with Dad the last time I was home. Everyone agreed, and Carol's daughters asked to read some memoirs of their own about their grandfather.

The day came to lay Dad to rest. It was bright and clear that day, very similar to the last time I saw him alive. I thought how perfect a day it would have been for Dad to sit on the porch and watch the world pass by; today it was passing without him. Close friends and family visited the funeral home and paid their last respects to Dad. The funeral director asked us if we wanted to leave any mementoes in the casket, touch him, or kiss him one last time before he closed the coffin. My nephew, John, placed into the casket a Santa Claus ornament that he'd made in the first grade as a Christmas present for his grandfather. Dad had kept the ornament all this time, and John had asked his grandmother if he could have it back. He wanted it back so he could place it in his grandfather's hands. He opened his hand, put the ornament inside, and said, "This was for you, and I love you, Poppa." His granddaughter, Kate, placed a quarter in his other hand. It was a tradition that Dad would always give his granddaughters twenty-five cents in case they need to call him for any reason.

Leaning over the casket and kissing him on his forehead one last time, I softly whispered, "Good-bye, Dad. I love you!" I barely had the words out of my mouth when Dad's words echoed in my ear: *Be strong. You're the new leader of this family.* A façade of strength masked my face as I took a deep breath and attempted to console my mother.

Mom began to tremble and suddenly burst into tears as they closed the casket for the last time. She knew this was it, the end of fifty-six years of marriage; good, bad, or otherwise, it was finally over. As I watched her cry, during what may have been her most painful hour, I wondered, why? Why had we, or anyone else for that matter, tolerated my dad's behavior for so long? So many thoughts were racing through my brain that it became almost surreal.

I felt like I was in another place and another time. I grasped my wife's hand and glanced at her with an expression that begged, "Please don't let this happen! This can't be happening." I looked at the American flag draped over the casket and thought, *This can't be my dad; he's too strong and powerful to pass away. This only happens to other people.*

In a daze, we left the funeral home for the church, and the limousine ride was quiet except for the sound of sniffles. We pulled up to the same small Catholic church where Mom and Dad had ecstatically stood at the top of the granite stairs when they were married. I recalled the photos that Mom had shown me many years ago, in which they posed outside the church that day.

I held Mom's hand as we sat in the front pew and patiently waited for friends and family to arrive. It felt like hours, but it was only a matter of minutes. As the service began, I looked over my shoulder and saw that the church was filled with family and close friends.

As the service continued, our nieces, Kris and Meg, stepped up to the podium and spoke of their memories of their Poppa. They had much to say and recalled the good times they'd had with their grandfather. Katie was more sentimental, remaining seated and silent but gasping for breath as she wept.

I maintained my composure well, and it was now time for me to address our dad, family, and friends. Rising to my feet, I could feel my heart race faster and faster; my mouth and throat became parched, and my palms were sweaty. I walked past the casket and the altar to the podium. I made eye contact with my mother and paused for a moment. The church became quiet and still. I faced everyone, took a deep breath, and told myself I could do this. Standing at the podium wearing my desert camouflage uniform, just as Dad had requested on that very first visit, I proceeded to read the short story I'd written about him in June. It was extremely difficult not only for me but for anyone under the circumstances.

This lieutenant colonel had addressed generals, the secretary of defense, and the surgeon general of the army; but addressing my dad under these conditions was an enormous task, one that I was determined to complete with pride and respect. I had to fulfill this task with the strength and courage that everyone knew me for, especially my dad. For whatever reason, I wanted to prove to my father one last time that I was strong and determined like him but at the same time very different from him.

As I read the story, I stood tall and proud, with my shoulders back and my head up. The weeping and crying that echoed through the church didn't make it any easier for me, but I continued to read. I wanted my dad to be proud of what I had to say about him. I also wanted everyone in the church to know about my cherished last day with my dad.

My intention was to create a new memory of my father, to give us a new past and a fresh beginning. There were no mixed emotions as I read the story; the past was gone, and in its place was a renewed sense of hope and forgiveness.

Throughout my life, I'd always been able to forgive but not forget. Later, I was able to forget but not forgive. Never during those years had I been able to do both at the same time. It was like those two parallel lines you learn about in geometry class, stretching out forever but never meeting.

That day, I forgave.

That day, I forgot.

It was a day for looking backward and moving forward. It was a day for grieving but also for leaving the grief behind. In those moments at the podium, my dad came alive through my story, my words, my images, and my memories. He gave me life, and through words, I gave him life. Our roles had reversed again, and for once, I welcomed the feeling of paying my father the ultimate tribute.

I felt a sense of relief, a sense of accomplishment, and a sense of making final peace with my father. In military fashion, I walked directly up to his American flag-draped casket, came to attention, and rendered him his final salute.

It was the ultimate symbol of respect, a greeting between comrades, not enemies. With that salute, I buried the past and forgave the man who, for better or worse, had given me life and forged this very soldier in uniform who now stood before his casket.

The final leg of my dad's journey was to the cemetery, with full military honors. As the first shots rang out from the twenty-one-gun salute in honor of Corporal Edgar "Jack" Gouin, U.S. Army veteran, I flinched. I was still gun-shy from the combat zone, and my recent memories started to take me back to Mosul. I knew I'd have to return and finish what I'd volunteered for eight months ago.

It seemed I'd done this only a few weeks ago, with my sister taking me back to the airport; but this time, I had the memory of our father. The trip back to Iraq was long and tedious, and I had four months remaining in my tour of duty. I needed to prepare myself mentally for what I'd agreed to do, above all to be a good soldier.

I eventually awoke to my hot, sandy reality as the Blackhawk helicopter approached the helipad for a landing in Mosul. I was back in Iraq and back to the war on terrorism, as though I'd never left. I was still drenched with sweat from head to toe and had one final thought before resuming another battle. I began to think about what was ahead of me in the next several months and how my family was going to cope and adjust to life without Dad back home.

We can no more choose our families than we can choose our battles.

As a son, I'd always thought my father was evil; as a soldier, I'd always looked upon my service as a duty rather than an opportunity. Now, I could see the world through my father's eyes, and I realized that by continuing to hate my father all those years I'd only ended up hurting myself.

Only in the years after forgiveness and rebuilding had we truly come to a place of peace in our relationship; only by being tested by battle and finding ourselves frail and human did we discover the strength to enter a new territory and end the skirmish that had dominated our private war.

Forgiveness is not a debt that we owe our parents; it is a right we earn through perseverance and maturity. For centuries, the salute has meant many things to many people. It is a sign of courtesy, respect, duty, honor, allegiance, service, passion, and patriotism.

For me, on that fateful day, it was all of the above. I'd like to think my dad would agree.

Epilogue

My mother now enjoys living with Carol during the cool Rhode Island summers and with me during the moderate Texas winters. She has resumed painting and sketching seascapes, her childhood dream, in the warm Texas sun. She often has dreams about her husband and continues to love him dearly to this day.

Carol continues watching over her wonderful family, including her children, grandchildren, and husband, Bill, at home in Woonsocket, Rhode Island.

Michael happily lives in a small town outside of Woonsocket with his wife of over twenty-five years; he has grandchildren. He has worked for Amtrak for over thirty years.

My office staff is happy that I've safely returned from Iraq, and we've resumed our great working relationship. Although I have struggled over the past three years to revive my practice to pre-deployment patient levels, I am determined it will succeed. The field of medicine is quite unforgiving for a sole practitioner in a private practice. Taking a one-year break and returning is like starting a practice all over again. It will take me another year to recover completely from the deployment.

The deployment to Iraq and coping with my return placed a severe strain on my once-beautiful relationship. Today I am divorced, but I stand firm in my conviction that I did the right thing by going to Iraq. My deployment gave me an entirely new outlook on life, and, for once, I felt a true sense of worth by helping others who needed help, especially my fellow soldiers. Many service members and their families have made the ultimate sacrifice. Their reasons for going into the military and deploying may vary, but the common goal is freedom. I do not consider my military service or deployment a sacrifice but merely a temporary hardship, a bump in the road. I raised my hand willingly thirty years ago, fully understanding that the military is designed for war, regardless of the benefits it may offer. There should be no doubt in anybody's mind that when you join the military you are preparing for war during peace.

I was not blessed by God with children, but I know in my heart that I learned from the mistakes of my father. If given the chance, I would be a great parent with an enormous amount of love to share. Sometimes we wish we could have a second chance at life. It was difficult as a child to tell my dad that I loved him, and rarely did I hear it from him. But as I grew older, I knew that opportunities to tell him would become less and more limited until that fateful day.

Despite my father's behavior, I still love and miss him today!

About the Author

Dr. John R. Gouin grew up in a low-income neighborhood in Woonsocket, Rhode Island, a small city of mostly French Canadian immigrants that had a large textile industry in the late 1800s and early 1900s. He was a star high school and college athlete until he sustained a devastating injury that destroyed any opportunity for a professional football career.

He received his undergraduate degree from the University of Rhode Island and his doctorate in podiatric medicine degree from Scholl College in Chicago, Illinois. He completed his residency in foot and ankle surgery at Loretto Hospital and Hugar Foot and Ankle Center in Chicago as well. Dr. Gouin has practiced podiatry in Corpus Christi, Texas for the past eighteen years and is a board-certified foot surgeon with Corpus Christi Podiatry Associates. He has returned to private practice since his release from active duty in 2006.

He served his country honorably for over thirty-three years and continues that service today as a colonel in the United States Army Reserves. He is now the commander of the 228th Combat Support Hospital in San Antonio, Texas. He is a distinguished military graduate from the University of Rhode Island ROTC program. He is a graduate of the Special Forces Course, AMEDD Officer Basic, Advanced Course, and Combat Casualty Care Course at Fort Sam, Houston, Texas. He completed the Combined Armed Services and Staff School and the Army Command and General Staff College, Fort Leavenworth, Kansas.

Dr. Gouin returned to the United States after volunteering to serve one year on active duty in Tikrit and Mosul, Iraq, for Operation Iraqi Freedom.

He was a special staff officer, medical operations officer, and foot surgeon while assigned to the 228th Combat Support Hospital in Iraq with his home station San Antonio, Texas.

Col. Gouin's personal awards and decorations include the Bronze Star Medal; Meritorious Service Medal with Oak Leaf Cluster; Army Commendation Medal with Oak Leaf Cluster; Army Achievement Medal; Army Good Conduct Medal; Army Reserve Components Achievement Medal; National Defense Service Medal with Bronze Star Device; Iraqi Campaign Medal; Global War on Terrorism Service Medal; Armed Forces Reserve Medal with "M" Device; Army Service Ribbon; Special Forces Tab; Combat Action Badge; Expert Infantry Badge; Parachute Badge; Army Meritorious Unit Citation; and Army Superior Unit Award.

An Unforgettable Salute is his first project and has taken approximately three years to write. He was inspired to write this book while serving in Iraq, which changed his life forever. He has several other great book ideas that are currently in progress.

The Diamondback
LTC John R. Gouin

HHD 228TH CSH
MOSUL, IRAQ
john.gouin@us.army.mil

Volume I Issue 3
July 2005

An Unforgettable Salute

Recently, I was called home from Iraq for an Emergency Leave to visit my father, who is seriously ill. Leaving my parents and returning to Iraq will be a day never forgotten. It was a solemn morning and mostly quiet around the house. Mother was limping with pain from her severe arthritis and several knee surgeries. She is a very tough and stubborn woman. Dad was sitting outside on the porch enjoying the beautiful New England weather. I was packing my luggage preparing to leave for a 2 o'clock flight back to Iraq. Denise, my wife, was very helpful getting things in order. My sister, Carol, planned to bring me to the airport, despite her reluctance and sadness to see me return.

I remember walking out the back door onto the porch and Dad was sitting in his rocking chair with a cowboy hat on. He appeared somewhat comfortable. He did not appear in pain. I sat in the chair next to him and began to cry. I told him repeatedly that I loved him and kissed his hand and kissed his hand and kissed his hand. I told him I wanted him to be proud of me and he replied he always has. He asked me to be strong as I always have been and that I was the new leader of this family. As we said our goodbyes, he said "so long" as he always has because he never wanted to say "goodbye." I told him "Dad, don't you go and die on me. You have to wait until I come home because if you do I'll never talk to you again." He said "if I do you'll kill me won't you?" We laughed a little bit; I gave him a big hug and kissed him on his forehead, then walked back into the house. I noticed on my way back in that my sister must have overheard our conversation and was crying as well. As I collected my bags I looked at my wife and told her that that was the most difficult thing I have ever done. The tears were streaming down my face. I grabbed my bags and walked out the front door to Carol's car. I attempted to catch my breath and stop crying but I could not keep back the tears.

Walking out the front door to the car, I felt an uncanny presence of someone watching me. I turned and noticed my Dad standing on the back deck. We made eye contact and he rendered me a salute. I proudly came to the position of attention and returned the honor and professional courtesy. That salute will always be the most important salute in my life and military career.

We loaded into the car and as we drove away, my Dad was looking over the porch and waving. I looked at my wife, grasped her hand and said to her "this is the toughest day of my life and I will never forget it."

The drive to the airport was quick but we knew what we had to do. Checking in with the ticket agent, we mentioned that I was returning to Iraq. The agent suggested under the circumstances my family may visit with me to the gate. We were extremely grateful and thankful she gave us the last hour together before boarding the aircraft. An hour went by and it was time for me to leave. I gave my usual bear hugs and told them not to worry about me because I am a good soldier and most of all just plain lucky. Thinking back to my Dad's request, I held back the tears and presented a facade of being strong. As I walked to the gate and began to ascend down the jet bridge, I turned, smiled and gave one last goodbye before my long journey back to Iraq

SUNNY AND HOT!

I never thought that I would consider a cold front at 103°F. It actually felt somewhat cool at that temperature early this morning. Of course that didn't last long and the temperature now is approaching 115°F. The usual daily temperature is approximately 120-125°F and I have seen it as high has 130°+F. So complaining about the heat in Corpus Christi is no longer going to happen. I will consider it a blessing to sit in my pool with the outside temperature at 90-100° F with an umbrella drink under my palms.

Breinigsville, PA USA
08 February 2011
255154BV00002B/12/P